TWENTIETH CENTURY INTERPRETATIONS
OF

KING LEAR

TWENTIETH CENTURY INTERPRETATIONS
OF

KING LEAR

A Collection of Critical Essays

Edited by
JANET ADELMAN

Prentice-Hall, Inc.   A SPECTRUM BOOK   *Englewood Cliffs, N.J.*

Library of Congress Cataloging in Publication Data
Main entry under title:

TWENTIETH CENTURY INTERPRETATIONS OF KING LEAR.

(Twentieth century interpretations)   (A Spectrum
Book)
    Bibliography: p.
    1. Shakespeare, William, 1564-1616.   King Lear.
2. Lear, King—Legends—History and criticism—
Addresses, essays, lectures.   I. Adelman, Janet.
PR2819.T9   822.3'3   77-14483
ISBN 0-13-516195-9
ISBN 0-13-516187-8 pbk.

10 9 8 7 6 5 4 3 2 1

PRENTICE-HALL INTERNATIONAL, INC., *London*
PRENTICE-HALL OF AUSTRALIA PTY. LIMITED, *Sydney*
PRENTICE-HALL OF CANADA, LTD., *Toronto*
PRENTICE-HALL OF INDIA PRIVATE LIMITED, *New Delhi*
PRENTICE-HALL OF JAPAN, INC., *Tokyo*
PRENTICE-HALL OF SOUTHEAST ASIA PTE. LTD., *Singapore*
WHITEHALL BOOKS LIMITED, *Wellington, New Zealand*

To Bob,
for his quick eye and ear, and his endless patience

Contents

TWENTIETH CENTURY INTERPRETATIONS
OF

KING LEAR

Introduction

by Janet Adelman

King Lear is an unusually harrowing experience for its audience, not only because of the nature of the experiences that it portrays, and its portrayal of them in an unusually intense way, but also because of its insistence on our sympathetic participation in them. It rarely leaves us safely distanced in the role of spectator; in fact the very process of our own spectatorship often seems to be at issue in the play. Even our literal sight is challenged. In a play in which sight and blindness are so significant, it is striking that the most visually exacting setting is in fact invisible, and serves to baffle the power of our eyes. Edgar's description of Dover Cliff has a visual density nowhere else apparent in the play: a density created in great part by Edgar's insistence on the limitations of sight, on things "almost too small for sight."[1] And indeed, our sight fails to guide us here. Faced with the bare flat stage, and accustomed to believing Shakespeare when he tells us where we are, we will see the cliff as Gloucester does, with our ears; but Gloucester's suspicion that the ground is flat, combined with our disinclination to believe that Edgar would allow his father to commit suicide, will simultaneously make us distrust our normal modes of stage vision. As Gloucester prepares to jump, the uncertain status of the cliff in our mind's eye allows us to participate sympathetically in Gloucester's farewell even as we reserve judgment: the cliff invisible to him is also invisible to us, but nonetheless vividly present to us both. The reality of the cliff becomes more suspect when Edgar tells us just before the farewell that he is trifling with his father's despair in order to cure

---

[1]*King Lear*, edited by Russell Fraser (New York, Toronto, London: New American Library, Signet Books, 1973), IV. vi. 20. All subsequent citations of the text are to this edition. My debt to previous Shakespeare criticism is too great to permit detailed acknowledgement. Readers of the essays below will often be aware of the nature and extent of this debt. My greatest single debt is to Maynard Mack, whose insight into Shakespeare and wise teaching provided me with the basis for the explorations in this essay.

it; but we do not understand the exact nature of this trifling until after Gloucester's fall, when Edgar allows us to see clearly with him for the first time in the scene. The cliff is fictitious; the flat stage is indeed flat; we can trust our eyes and rest assured that Gloucester is not dead. But we are immediately robbed of this certainty of perception, as Edgar realizes with increasing fear the danger of his trifling with despair: the cliff that exists only in "conceit" (ours and Gloucester's, as well as Edgar's) may prove fatal to Gloucester after all. Our uncertainty about the reality of the cliff is exchanged for uncertainty about its imaginative force: and the cliff again becomes visible to us, now as an emblem of the distance that Gloucester has fallen and of his bewilderment and despair. The uncertainties thrust on us by sight complement those thrust on Gloucester by blindness, and they allow us to participate in the larger uncertainties of the scene and especially to tolerate the ambiguity of Edgar's summary statement, "Thy life's a miracle" (IV. vi. 55): there is no miracle in surviving no fall from no cliff, and Edgar's statement seems more expressive of his own need to enforce a kindly interpretation on the brutal events of the universe than it is of the genuinely miraculous; but at the same time, since we as well as Gloucester have experienced the cliff from which he fell, and since we are newly weaned from the commonsense perception that an unreal cliff can do no harm, we will be inclined to believe that Gloucester's life, no matter how unwillingly maintained, is indeed a miracle not of physical but of psychical endurance. The dependence of this scene on the challenge it presents to our own sight is characteristic of the play: we are often told to "look there" at things invisible to us; and this insistence on the limitations of our sight usually acts to insure our participation in the inner experience of the characters. The intense inner reality of Poor Tom's fiends ("There could I have him now—and there—and there again—and there"—III. iv. 61-62) or of Regan's escape from Lear's judgment ("Stop her there!"—III. vi. 53) is brought home to us precisely because we cannot see them. But at the end of the play, the limitations of our sight act to exclude us from Lear's experience and to unite us with those who watch him. We strain, with Kent and Edgar, to see what Lear asks us to see in the dead body of his daughter ("Do you see this? Look on her. Look, her lips,/ Look there, look there"—V. iii. 312-13), but we see only the distance by which his experience has exceeded ours, and know that we "shall never see so much" (V. iii. 328). We are left with the desolation caused by our knowledge that Lear's vision, and he himself, have passed beyond us.

Moments like these, in which the limitations of our literal sight become part of the experience of the play, may serve us as emblems for that collapse of the distance between spectator and participant toward which the play moves; for in fact both the possibilities and limitations of the role of spectator are explored within the play itself. The figure of Edgar, for example, is curiously suspended between the roles of spectator and participant; although he is one of the main characters in the play, and one of those who suffers most brutally, he nonetheless seems more often to be a spectator than an actor. Despite his disclaimer in the final line, he has surely, in a literal sense, seen more than any of the other characters: he is spectator to Lear's madness on the heath, his father's suicide attempt, the meeting between his father and Lear, Lear's great agony at the death of Cordelia and, finally, Lear's own death. If we believe in his disclaimer, that he has not seen so much as Gloucester and Lear, we do so because they have seen more deeply than he has. Indeed, his very role as spectator has allowed him some measure of detachment from what he has seen throughout the play, even from his own most immediate pain: he watches his transformation into Poor Tom and comments on his performance as a Bedlam beggar almost as though he were a critical member of the audience; he emerges from his role as Poor Tom to meditate in extraordinarily abstract terms on his feelings and his predicament (III. vi. 101-14). Lear calls Edgar/ Poor Tom "my philosopher" (III. iv. 179) partly because he seems to be the thing itself and hence able to teach about the unaccommodated life in its purest form; but Edgar gains his title as the play's philosopher not through his immersion in experience but through his attempts to escape from it. He tries more insistently than any other character to gain some distance on suffering, and hence relief from it, by making it conform to a comprehensible pattern. His disquisition on the tendency of things to get better (IV. i. 1-9), interrupted only by the appearance of his newly blinded father, is the extreme example of this attempt and amply illustrates its dangers. We may recognize the poignant human necessity that underlies such moments, and nonetheless recognize in them a model of the dangers inherent in the role of spectator, and perhaps especially in the role of critic: the comforting distance that comes from the sheer processes of intellection, of gaining control over events and feelings by understanding them, may allow us to evade the experience altogether. For Edgar's danger is our own: we console ourselves by placing some sort of intellectual pattern or formula between the event and the self.[2] (Even a conclusion as bleak as Gloucester's "As flies to wanton boys"—a conclusion readily embraced by many critics who therefore congratulate themselves on the steely realism of their vision—can be consoling insofar as it makes experience comprehensible and thus tolerable: no surprises here.) But if Edgar is our model for a kind of spectatorship that allows us to escape from experience, he is also our model for a kind of spectatorship that admits the fullness of the experience before us, without denying it or attempting to distance ourselves: the kind of spectatorship toward which the play impels us if we are open to it. That Edgar is so prone to using his role as spectator as a means of escaping experience makes particularly poignant those moments in which this very role involves him inescapably in the reality and the pain of the events that he witnesses: "I would not take this from report: it is,/ And my heart breaks at it" (IV. vi. 143-44). Edgar's response to the meeting of Lear and his father merges his pain as spectator with the pain that they are suffering: "O thou side-piercing sight!" (IV. vi. 85) he cries, in words that suggest a Christ-like compassion—literally *feeling with*—for the sorrows of mankind, and of the particular men in front of him.

And this *feeling with* is what the play demands of us as spectators. As we watch the moment in which Cornwall blinds Gloucester, for instance, we cannot help but be reminded of the vulnerability of our own eyes, and our dependence on them; the peculiar horror of Cornwall's "Out, vile jelly" (III. vii. 84) lies partly in the vividness with which it recalls to us the consistency, and hence the fragility, of the human eye, so that we feel our eyes imperilled as well as Gloucester's. (Many of us close our eyes to avoid the sight, thus momentarily reduplicating Gloucester's experience of darkness.) Here the role of spectator is no sure bulwark against pain; and in feeling for ourselves, we feel with Gloucester. The play everywhere insists on the interdependence of feeling for self and fellow-feeling, and on the necessity of both for true sight. At the moment that Lear most poignantly becomes spectator to his own pain, he teaches us the interdependence of feeling for self and for another: "I should ev'n die with pity,/ To see another thus" (IV. vii. 53-54).

---

[2]This is by no means to argue that "understanding" is not both a human necessity and one of our fundamental responsibilities to the play; it is merely to suggest some of the dangers inherent in "understanding" insofar as it allows us to escape from feeling, an even more primary human necessity and responsibility.

Lear's feeling for himself and his own vulnerability here spills out toward pity for another, and that pity returns to the self: the movement suggests that there can be no true fellow-feeling without feeling for the self and its vulnerabilities ("How dost, my boy? Art cold?/ I am cold myself"—III. ii. 68-69). The blinded Gloucester begins to see the world out of the intensity of his own pain; and his "I see it feelingly" (IV. vi. 151) thus becomes the model for our own spectatorship at its best. To see this play at all, we must be willing to open ourselves to feeling, lest we imitate Gloucester's lust-dieted man "that will not see/ Because he does not feel" (IV. i. 70-71). The play thus demands from us not only insight or understanding (with the suggestion of a measure of distance from the events we witness) but the willingness to make ourselves vulnerable to feeling. For we risk ourselves, admit our own vulnerabilities, in seeing this play feelingly; in fact, the ending of the play is tolerable at all partly because it gives us proof positive of the extent to which we are feeling human beings. We have watched Lear grow in feeling, until he dies, in Maynard Mack's beautiful phrase, "with his whole being launched toward another";[3] at the end we have not only the consolation of Lear's achievement but the consolation that we ourselves are so launched, that we would ev'n die of pity. The end of the play enlarges our awareness of the intensity of our own feelings, and thus brings us into the human community, or rather demonstrates to us how fully we are members of it. But it can do so only insofar as we are willing to risk ourselves.

On the face of it, the play seems to resist rather than to encourage our participation. In no other tragedy are we given so few of the seducing comforts that can lead us into the world of the play: a clear sense of the personality, motivation, or moral status of the major characters, for instance, or of the antecedents of the plot. In the other tragedies, even when our initial impressions prove treacherous, they serve to engage us with the play; but these characters simply explode on the stage with an energy whose sources we can only guess at. And as we are given no sense of their past, or of the past history of the actions we are witnessing, so we are given no sense of precise location in time. The play begins with a contemporary ease, but moves immediately into an apparently archaic ceremony that

[3]Maynard Mack, *King Lear in Our Time* (Berkeley and Los Angeles: The University of California Press, 1965), p. 100. See p. 57 in this volume.

seems to have nothing to do with Elizabethan political life, seems
in fact to insist on its distance from contemporary political concerns
by introducing the alarming spectacle of a king about to divide his
kingdom and then making it clear that the king's noblemen and
counsellors do not find the spectacle alarming. But if the setting is
not contemporary, neither is it safely fixed in an historical past;
there is no attempt to recreate an historical moment, with its re-
assurances: the Rome of *Julius Caesar,* for example, or of *Coriolanus.*
These characters are not Christians, but neither are they pagans of
a reassuringly familiar type: they swear by strange and alien gods,
not only by Hecate and Apollo, but by the sacred radiance of the sun.
As we watch the first scene unfold, we do not know where we are,
or among whom.

But precisely our disorientation is essential to the process by which
the play in fact engages us in its deepest concerns. For we come to
feel this unlocalized past of England as part of our own past, psychologically rather than historically: and hence as alive in our present selves. However foreign the setting, however motiveless the
actions, these events are familiar to us: familiar from our childhood,
when we knew all about the three daughters, and knew that the
scorned youngest was the best. The opening of *King Lear,* with its
elements of fairy tale, thus has its roots in the memories of our childhood and the knowledge we had then, knowledge that is primitive
and powerful because we feel it not as acquired or debatable, but as
part of ourselves. And because these characters are at once remote
and familiar, because they are unlocalized in time and unencum-
bered by those details of personal history that might serve to alienate
their concerns from our own, they seem to emerge from some unknown part of ourselves, as if in a dream; remote from our immediate
experience, they nonetheless recall us to ourselves, although ourselves writ large and seen in purer form. Indeed, the very myste-
riousness of the first scene demands our participation in it. Because
Shakespeare gives us no clear sense of why the characters act as they
do, we are forced to try to understand them in the only way available to us: we begin to understand them by understanding ourselves,
insofar as their dilemmas and responses confront us with our own.
We have all faced, in one way or another, the dilemma that faces
Lear's daughters. We have had to choose, with Cordelia, between a
dutiful display of love made meaningless because it is not freely
given, and a withholding of the display, a refusal to demean our
love by producing it on demand, as if for a reward. The first choice

will feel frighteningly insincere, and the second frighteningly nig-gardly, to us as to others; the first issues on stage in the radical in-sincerity of Goneril and Regan, the second in Cordelia's tendency to protect her own integrity at any cost. (Cordelia's dilemma is of course complicated and intensified by her particular situation: she is simultaneously fighting for the right to maintain the integrity of her own emotions and the right to a love separate from her love for her father. Hence her rather niggardly arithmetic of love: to have a love different in kind, and therefore legitimately sexual, for her husband, she must be able to imagine dividing her love in just the mechanical way that she suggests.) As we have faced the dilemma of the daughters, so we have faced the anxieties that prompt Lear's question: the desire to control exactly that which loses its value once it is not given freely is partly an attempt to repair the damage of our first fall, the first recognition of the separation of self and other that makes us so frighteningly aware of our dependence on everything that is outside of ourselves, everything we find that we cannot con-trol. Even the form of Lear's question suggests his attempt to repair this damage: he does not ask "Which of you doth love us most?" but "Which of you shall we say doth love us most?" as though the love of his daughters were contingent on his saying. (As the specifics of Cordelia's situation lend a particular urgency to her dilemma, so do those of Lear: insofar as he is about to become wholly dependent on his daughters, his need to assert radical control over them is intensified. He attempts to alleviate the sense of his dependence on them not only by demonstrating his control, but also by compelling their love through a system of barter, so that it becomes something he has purchased and hence has a right to possess, not something spontaneously given and hence outside his control. It will later be the thought of filial ingratitude that drives him to madness [III. iv. 14-22] because he has placed all his sense of his own power, his only bulwark against a terrifying admission of dependency and helpless-ness, in a system of tit-for-tat. The failure of this defensive system leads him to question the whole of justice, human and divine, until Cordelia's "no cause" [IV. vii. 75] releases him from its confines.)

We understand these characters at the start partly insofar as we allow their dilemmas to find echoes within us; and we are encouraged to participate in their psychic lives by those very elements that make *King Lear* seem remote to us, and removed from our ordinary ways of understanding. This point is worth belaboring because it is so often assumed that the accurate representation of psychological

states is inevitably dependent on a naturalistic mode of characterization; and in its worthy effort to emphasize the degree to which
Shakespeare presents his characters emblematically or symbolically
as well as naturalistically, criticism after Bradley has sometimes
tended to declare psychological questions off-bounds and therefore
to minimize the extraordinary psychological power of Shakespeare's
plays. It is of course undeniable that Shakespeare's relative indif-
ference to naturalism does not always allow for a psychological
realism naturalistically conceived, that is, for the realistic presentation of psychological processes as they have their genesis and
development in everyday life. But it seems to me equally undeniable
that Shakespeare often achieves psychological realism of another
kind: truth to states of heart and mind that make perfect sense to us
although we are not given their day-by-day genesis, and although
we never see them in pure form in our friends and neighbors. We
are not told the process by which Lear gets into the state in which we
find him in Act I; but we recognize the state when we see it. And in
fact an emblematic presentation of character may serve to express
this kind of psychological realism at least as well as a naturalistic
one; we need think only of Spenser's portrayal of Despair, or of
Amoret entrapped by Busirane. Furthermore, the argument that the
presentation of a character at a particular moment is not naturalistic
but emblematic is sometimes vitiated by the uses to which it is put:
for it is often invoked at precisely those moments when the character
might otherwise be suspected of unbecoming behavior or of an inconsistency painful to us. But however useful this argument may
sometimes be, we should not invoke it to get the character off the
hook, or to rescue ourselves from uncomfortable perceptions and
questions. For the questions that are thus declared off-bounds may
indicate more about the assumptions that we wish to preserve about
a particular character, or about character in general, than they do
about the shifts in Shakespeare's mode of presenting character.

The absolute goodness and nobility of Edgar, for example, has
been assumed in much of the criticism of the twentieth century,
perhaps partly because in a play in which the wicked are so palpably
and purely wicked, we long to find the good as palpably and purely
good. (We thus make the play easier for ourselves to endure, since
both the wickedness and the goodness in it become inhuman alternatives, beyond our range.) But Edgar's absolute goodness can be
assumed only at the price of overlooking certain questions raised by
his behavior: and our best warrant for overlooking them is a concept

of character that allows us to declare that, at certain moments, Edgar takes on an emblematic quality that absolves him from the ordinary responsibilities of human beings. Why, for example, does Edgar conceal his identity from his father for so long that he himself begins to feel that his behavior was at fault (V. iii. 194)? Bethell believes that we simply should not ask: Shakespeare does not give us an explanation because, "in the treatment of Edgar, propriety on the plane of naturalism yields to the needs of symbolic expression";[4] we will presumably raise the question only insofar as we are inattentive to Shakespeare's shifts of mode. Why does Edgar refer so brutally to the divine justice manifest in his father's blinding? For Mack, Edgar's affinities with figures from the morality plays account amply for the harshness of his pronouncement:

> His unblinking attitude toward his father's transgressions and his strict code of retribution...are less (one must think) characteristics of the solicitous and patient guide of Gloucester and the pitying observer of Lear than necessities of his role as presenter of legitimacy and polar opposite to his brother's Appetite.[5]

But it is difficult for an audience to split its responses in this way; and is there really any less reason for us to respond to Edgar's harshness here than to his pity earlier? Richly conceived characters are as capable of inconsistency and emotional complexity as the human beings to whom they are distantly related; and we run the risk of impoverishing them unnecessarily if we allow our criteria of consistency to determine for us which emotions are appropriate to whom, and consequently which emotions we will choose to accept as truly theirs. In the case of these lapses on Edgar's part, Bradley's relatively uncomplicated comments may be preferable to the explantations of his more sophisticated followers: he confronts squarely the ways in which these moments make us uncomfortable.[6] His

---

[4]S. L. Bethell, *Shakespeare and the Popular Dramatic Tradition* (Durham: Duke University Press, 1944), p. 77.

[5]Mack, *King Lear in Our Time*, p. 61. For a fuller account of Mack's views of Shakespearean character, see pp. 113-14 in this volume.

[6]A. C. Bradley, *Shakespearean Tragedy* (London: Macmillan and Co., Ltd., 1904), pp. 258, 305-6. It is interesting that, in the case of the second lapse, Bradley raises the possibility that Shakespeare "merely wished to introduce this moral somehow, and did not mean the speech to be characteristic of the speaker" only to reject it; he believes that the speech is characteristic of Edgar, and connects it with his "pronounced and conscious religiousness" (pp. 305-306).

method has the virtue of leaving our response intact, without suggesting that it is the result of something wrong in us, something that
we can be educated not to feel. If we are taught thus to distrust our own responses, especially
when they seem to be firmly grounded in the text, is there not a
danger that the play will lose its most fundamental connection with
us? We should of course be aware of the ways in which Shakespeare's
purposes and the premises of his age may differ from our own. But
the request that we abandon the psychological mode of inquiry and
response at just those moments when the behavior of a character
seems unaccountable or bothersome to us is fundamentally a request
that we abandon an important part of ourselves; and as such, it will
often impoverish our experience of the play. Nor need we choose
between an emblematic and a psychological response to a particular
moment. If we are responding fully, we will respond to Edgar as
emblematic of something larger than himself when he announces
his new identity as "A most poor man, made tame to fortune's blows;/
Who, by the art of known and feeling sorrows,/ [Is] pregnant to good
pity" (IV. vi. 224-26): his new presence will epitomize for us the
beneficent sympathy of creatures for one another that has begun to
emerge in the play, and, specifically, the tutoring by fortune that
both Lear and Gloucester have undergone. But at the same time, we
should not be asked to deny the part of ourselves that responds to
Edgar's words as the culmination of an interchange between a particular son and his father, especially because the text itself seems to
insist on this response as well. Immediately after Lear and Gloucester
have recognized one another, Edgar and Gloucester seem to hover
on the brink of their own recognition scene:

> *Edgar.*   Well pray you, father.
> *Gloucester.* Now, good sir, what are you?
> *Edgar.* A most poor man, made tame to fortune's blows....
>
> (IV. vi. 222-24)

Edgar himself elicits Gloucester's question by calling him "father";[7]
but a moment later he avoids the opportunity to identify himself.
The intensity of Gloucester's desire to see Edgar in his touch (IV. i.
23), the proximity of this moment to the Lear-Gloucester recogni-

---

[7]Edgar calls Gloucester "thou happy father" immediately after Gloucester's fall
(IV. vi. 72), but there the word "father" provokes no questions because the surrounding phrase insures that it will not be understood literally: one would scarcely refer
to one's father as "thou father."

tion scene (and, once we have the benefit of hindsight, to the great recognition of father and daughter which follows almost immediately), and particularly Edgar's own wavering all serve to focus our attention on the inner state of father and son. And with our attention thus focused, we may be able to feel the movement of Edgar's hesitancy here, even if we cannot fully explain it: for he seems to wish to *be recognized* by his father (as Lear has been recognized); and this very wish compels him not to *reveal himself.*[8] This highly charged moment is an emblem not only for the moral truths of the play but for a particular state of mind; and recognition of Edgar's status as moral emblem need in no way impair our acknowledgment of his psychological state, and of the poignance of this moment for father and son.

As we watch Edgar become the most poor man made pregnant to good pity, indeed, as we watch him take on each of his new identities, we should be simultaneously aware of the use that the play makes of the new character who suddenly appears on stage and the use that Edgar himself makes of the new disguise, with the new potentialities for the self that it releases. The simultaneous awareness of his emblematic function and his inner state demanded of us by this moment is characteristic of the demands that Edgar makes on us throughout the play. Because the distance between Edgar's nature as emblem and his inner state often seems vast, because, that is, his various roles seem less well integrated than those of the other characters, Edgar poses the problem of simultaneous awareness particularly acutely; our understanding of him will consequently be an index to our understanding both of the play as a whole and of the possibilities inherent in Shakespeare's mode of characterization, here and elsewhere.

In the theater, I think, we have no trouble responding to Edgar as though he had an underlying self that emerged in different ways at different times. But many critics find Edgar's succession of emblematic disguises grounds for suspicion that he has no self; despite

[8]It is specifically his not revealing himself for which Edgar later castigates himself: "Never—O fault!—revealed myself unto him" (V. iii. 194). If we are sensitive to Edgar's refusal to reveal himself here, we will be less taken aback by his immediate plunge into a second new identity as Oswald approaches: his taking on the dialect of a peasant at this moment presents us with an important emblem of a social world that is beginning to find its strength at the bottom; but it simultaneously insures that Edgar's father will not recognize the trick of Edgar's voice as he has Lear's.

the prominence accorded him by the text, they tend to consider him not as a major character but as a whole host of minor characters, choric in function. And indeed, Edgar's central disguise as Poor Tom is so powerfully conceived that Poor Tom tends to become a character in his own right; it is in fact essential to the play that he be allowed to do so. The chaos of mad fragments to which Shakespeare submits his audience as well as Lear in Act III would lose its force if we were able to think of Poor Tom as only a disguise throughout Act III, scenes iv and vi; the hell-fiends that he looses into the play would cease to haunt us were we to bear constantly in mind that they are merely the protective coloring of a perfectly sane earl's son; and the compassion for the poor that we and Lear feel at the center of this world would be at least partly displaced by the ironic recognition that this is no ordinary madman and beggar but a fallen nobleman. Shakespeare frequently reminds us that Poor Tom is Edgar; but Poor Tom's ability to absorb us into his madness and misery means that we greet each reappearance of Edgar with slight surprise. For the play demands from us a kind of doubleness of vision here, similar to the doubleness of vision demanded of us during the scene of Gloucester's leap: as we simultaneously believe and disbelieve in the independent existence of the cliff there, we believe and disbelieve in the independent existence of Poor Tom here.

The distinction between Edgar and Poor Tom could not, on the face of it, be clearer, even after Edgar has been reduced to circumstances not enormously different from Poor Tom's. Since Edgar and Poor Tom temporarily inhabit the same body, language is the chief means by which each is identified for the audience. And when Edgar resumes his own voice, and hence his own presence, for the first time at length, in the soliloquy concluding Act III, scene vi, his language is at the furthest possible remove from Poor Tom's: the dense particularity and wild prose of Poor Tom's language are replaced by Edgar's philosophic abstractions and his tightly controlled couplets. Edgar thus reminds us—and perhaps himself—that he is not Poor Tom; indeed, his language serves to characterize him for the audience as one who is in control of his emotions and to some extent of his situation, in sharp contrast to Poor Tom, who is frighteningly out of control. Nonetheless, it may not surprise us that these linguistic extremes inhabit one body: for they seem oddly dependent on one another. The orderly abstraction of Edgar's language is the necessary control for the apparently random particularity of Poor Tom's; and the mad freedom of Poor Tom's language is the necessary release from the overly rigid order of Edgar's. Neither extreme alone is a fully human language; taken together, they provide the widest possible expressive range. Each supplements the other, and between them, they serve as a way of tolerating the intolerable. And in fact, the very contrast between linguistic styles that serves to distinguish Poor Tom and Edgar for the audience serves also to suggest the dynamics of the relationship between them. For Edgar's rage toward order seems to grow partly in response to Poor Tom's rage toward chaos: the Edgar who identifies himself through his voice at the end of Act III, scene vi is far more philosophical and controlled than the baffled young man we have met earlier. Edgar's participation in Poor Tom's nightmarish freedom from emotional constraint seems to call for particularly harsh measures in the attempt to regain control over the self. In the speech in which he reclaims his identity, he defines himself almost purely by his opposition to Poor Tom, not by his response to his own experiences: he constructs a world in which the consolations available to mind replace the specifics of bodily torment, where emotion is schematized and rationalized nearly out of existence, a world populated only by general truths and abstractions, not by the particulars that haunt Poor Tom. Although at the end of this speech Edgar treats Poor Tom as a familiar companion, nearly synonymous with himself, he never permits himself to acknowledge the ways in which Poor Tom's experience echoes his own. Indeed, the intensity of Edgar's effort toward sanity here, his attempt to distance himself utterly from Poor Tom, may make us uneasy: the degree to which this speech is out of touch with the reality of Edgar's experience, or with our experience of the scene we have just witnessed, make it appear more frightening and in some sense less sane than anything Lear or Poor Tom says.[9] Those critics who take the disintegrationist view of Edgar in fact have good precedent, since Edgar himself seems to want to view himself in discrete parts. His attempt to dissociate himself from his disguises is at one with his attempt to keep himself at a distance from his experiences, in effect to disown parts

[9]"When we our betters see bearing our woes" is the start of a meditation on woe that pluralizes it and robs it of its pain by suggesting that one woe is very much like another. But do we really feel that Edgar's woe is much like Lear's? Edgar's comment here seems to be the meditative and "sane" equivalent of Lear's mad greeting to Poor Tom: "What, has his daughters brought him to this pass?" (III. iv. 6 3)

of himself; he encourages us to treat him as a series of emblems because he himself is prone to treat his life as though it were a series of emblems.[10]

But the very firmness with which Edgar must separate himself from Poor Tom makes us wonder if the relationship between self and role is not more intimate than we had previously supposed. And in fact the nature of the disguise that Edgar chooses suggests that it is very much a part of him. Any disguise is of course prone to be seen as epitomizing something in the self, particularly in a world in which clothing is so symbolically significant. But a disguise in which one strips off all one's clothing is especially liable to affect us as a revelation of the self rather than a covering up of it. Edgar initially conceives of his disguise simply as a means to preserve himself: "I heard myself proclaimed,/ .... Whiles I may 'scape,/ I will preserve myself; and am bethought/ To take the basest and most poorest shape. ..." (II. iii. 1-7) But as he begins to imagine his role, he enters into it with increasing enthusiasm, enumerating the Bedlam's objects of self-torture and his habitats with a wild energy not unlike Poor Tom's own, finally even imitating his cries. And whatever Edgar's initial plans for keeping his role distinct from himself, the disguise forbids such distance: we may be sure that Edgar shivers when Tom's a-cold, and that the rosemary sprigs in Tom's arms hurt Edgar's as well. By the end of the transformation speech, the self that Edgar had thought to preserve intact through the process of disguise has been totally obliterated: "Edgar I nothing am." (II. iii. 21). As we watch Edgar becoming Poor Tom, as we watch the enthusiasm with which he embraces the vulnerability and even the self-inflicted pain of Poor Tom, we must feel that Poor Tom serves the needs of Edgar as well as those of the play. For the young man about whom we know so little both submerges himself and reveals himself in his disguise. We hear almost nothing directly about Edgar's emotional state, his reaction to his father's apparently inexplicable desire to kill him; but we watch him create in Poor Tom a creature through whom he can safely express his sense of helpless victimization, of utter vulnerability and confusion. And the efficacy of the role of Poor Tom for Edgar depends largely on Edgar's ability to claim that it is wholly separate from himself: Poor Tom, pursued by fiends as Edgar is pursued by his father, homeless as Edgar is newly homeless, allows Edgar to express these emotions as

[10]I am indebted to Susan Harris for this perception; conversations with her have frequently enriched my understanding of *King Lear*.

though they were his own, but at the same time to gain a measure of control over them insofar as he can distance himself from the role of Poor Tom at will. Emotions that might otherwise threaten to overwhelm him can thus be disowned and controlled even as they are allowed expression: they become part of his disguise, his very means for preserving himself. When Gloucester suddenly appears, the double function of the disguise for Edgar becomes especially clear. Edgar's fear, his sense of his father as a ubiquitous persecutor, his sense of his own fragility, all find expression in Poor Tom's response, at the same time as that response serves to conceal him from his father:

> This is the foul fiend Flibbertigibbet. He begins at curfew, and walks till the first cock. He gives the web and the pin, squints the eye, and makes the harelip; mildews the white wheat, and hurts the poor creature of earth.   (III. iv. 117-21)

Despite Edgar's attempt to keep himself separate from Poor Tom, the likeness between Edgar and Poor Tom is finally as striking as the difference. For characteristic of both is a passivity, a willingness to see oneself as victim (and indeed to be victim), which borders on the masochistic. Poor Tom sees himself as tormented and led astray by fiends, as tempted to suicide and plagued by powers within and without (so that even his own hunger signals the presence of a persecuting fiend). The terms of Edgar's universe are very different, but his position in it is not: in place of the tormenting fiends, he puts the just (and justifying) gods; he can act only insofar as he sees himself as their agent. The curious indirectness of his cure of his father's despair—very much against his father's will—seems to allow Edgar as well as Gloucester to imagine that the cure is the work of the clearest gods.[11] And part of our discomfort with Edgar's later proclamation that the gods are just lies not in the harshness of the judgment but in the extent to which he manages to make his own role in the death of his brother and the punishment of his father disappear by attributing both to an agency wholly outside himself;

[11]Although Gloucester is cured of the desire to commit suicide, he is by no means cured of the desire to die quickly. After his meeting with Lear, he prays that the gods will kill him quickly so that he will not again be tempted to kill himself. The entrance of Oswald almost immediately afterward must strike him as an answer to his prayers, one of the few vouchsafed in this play; he says to Oswald, "Now let thy friendly hand/ Put strength enough to 't" (IV. vi. 233-34). Edgar of course has to interfere with this remedy of the gods; we would after all hate him if he did not act to protect his father here.

that he does so immediately after killing his brother and immediately before expressing some guilt about his treatment of his father (V. iii. 194) suggests the protective function of this attribution. The same unwillingness to act on his own behalf, the same need to distance his actions from himself, may partly dictate Edgar's succession of disguises. Both of Edgar's decided actions—his killing of Oswald and his killing of Edmund—are performed in disguises that allow him to submerge himself in a role: the first under the protection of the role of the righteous peasant, the second under the double protection of his disguise as nameless noble and the distance from the self that ceremony affords.

If we have been attending to Edgar not merely as a succession of roles, but as a full character who expresses himself through these roles, we are aware that he is remarkably passive from the start. From the moment of Edmund's introduction of him—"and pat he comes, like the catastrophe of the old comedy" (I. ii. 145)—he tends to fall too easily into roles that others have created for him. Even his choice of the role of Poor Tom is anticipated by Edmund: that Edmund sighs like Tom o' Bedlam (I. ii. 147) long before Edgar does creates for us in theatrical terms the uncanny sense that Edmund has designed this role for Edgar too. From the start, Edgar is prey to events, the perfect foil for Edmund, who somewhat uneasily claims to control them.[12] It is a necessity of Edgar's own nature, not merely a necessity of the plot, that makes him so quick to accept Edmund's scenario and run away from his father's anger; and the same necessity is epitomized by the ease with which he takes on the role of the Bedlam beggar, who is defined less by what he does than by what he must endure. Even the speech in which Edgar attempts to reclaim his own character as distinct from Poor Tom's is dictated by this necessity: for his flight into shadowy abstractions allows him

[12]Edmund's delight in his machinations and his disbelief in astrology are symptoms of his status as a Renaissance version of the self-made man, who acknowledges no shaping agency outside of his own will. But at the same time, his initial claim that he is unchangeably what he is (I. ii. 142-43) suggests that he sees his own nature as given, ultimately outside his control; and in the end, he seems to view his life with a fatalism and a consequent denial of responsibility far more fundamental than Edgar's own (V. iii. 176). But his dropping of the pose of utter control over the self and events seems to allow him to change indeed, and to take on true responsibility as a moral agent despite his own nature (V. iii. 246), as though he can become fully human only when he can acknowledge his own helplessness. It is the final irony of this progression that his attempt to assert himself not as self-made man in control of events but as true moral agent is foiled by events beyond his control.

to create a world in which no action is necessary, in which action is in fact impossible. In this world, his pain is inflicted by the picture of nobody, not by father or brother, Flibbertigibbet or Frateretto, but by a "false opinion" (III. vi. 111) against whom he cannot possibly fight; and the same false opinion will effect his restoration when it repeals and reconciles him in his just proof, all without his own agency. Given Edgar's fear of action, his need to see himself as an agent of the just gods, we can begin to understand his unwillingness to take back his personal identity by acknowledging himself to his father until he senses that events outside himself are ready to confer that identity on him, that false opinion has begun the task of reconciling him. We can begin also to understand his need to be recognized rather than to reveal himself, and even the ways in which this desire forces him to be punitive not only to Gloucester but also to himself: if he denies Gloucester his eyes by refusing to reveal himself (IV. i. 24), he also denies himself the support that his father's love would give him. For Edgar's passive unwillingness to act on his own behalf turns ultimately against himself. Instead of attempting to disarm persecution, he embraces persecution: but he substitutes the persecution of the sky (II. iii. 12) for the more personal and hence more painful persecution of his father.[13] In his own person, Edgar never expresses direct anger against his father or even against the nameless villain whom he initially assumes has done him wrong (I. ii. 177); just when we might expect to see him expressing anger and the desire for revenge or self-justification, we see him stripping and inflicting pain on himself in the person of Poor Tom. If Lear is much too prone to placing blame outside himself, Edgar is unable to place blame at all: in him the desire to punish home is turned against the self. Characteristically, when Lear imagines fiends attacking his enemies, Edgar diverts this attack onto himself:

> *Lear.* To have a thousand with red burning spits
>   Come hizzing in upon 'em —
> *Edgar.* The foul fiend bites my back. (III. vi. 15-17)

The passivity and even the masochism of Poor Tom serve Edgar well: for by turning punishment against the self, he can avoid turning it against the world. And insofar as Edgar's fantasies can be

---

[13]Lear will similarly use the storm to shelter him, for a moment, from thoughts of his persecuting daughters. But this movement toward the impersonal is unusual for Lear, who promptly endows the storm with a human face.

released without danger in his role as Poor Tom, Poor Tom can help us understand Edgar's need for the protection afforded by his passivity and even by its turning against the self: action is dangerous because Edgar's own fantasies are too explosive. For Edgar seems to allow everything that he has had to suppress to be the good, the legitimate, son to emerge in his portrait of Poor Tom. Poor Tom is now led, tormented, tempted to suicide; but the past that Edgar invents for him is entirely active, filled with a kind of frenzy of self-serving lust and aggression. In the subterranean realms to which Edgar allows his imagination to descend in the service of the role of Poor Tom, action itself is corrupt and calls down instant retaliation on the actor. Indeed, Poor Tom's present passivity is the punishment for his past actions. A belief in retaliation of this kind is in fact a constant feature of Edgar's imagination: if Poor Tom is punished by the fiends for his act of darkness, Gloucester is punished by the just gods for his commerce with the dark and vicious place where Edmund was conceived. The danger implicit in action and the threat of retaliation are suggested by the odd song with which Edgar closes Act III, scene iv:

> Child Rowland to the dark tower came;
> His word was still, "Fie, foh, and fum,
> I smell the blood of a British man."   (III. iv. 185-87)[14]

The first line suggests the realm of heroic action and the entry into this realm of the young man on the point of attaining knighthood and hence maturity. The dark tower is in itself threatening; and the association of darkness with sexuality throughout the play may combine with the phallic suggestiveness of the tower to present an image of specifically sexual threat for the young man about to enter manhood. At this point the implicit pun on "child" seems to act as the focus for the anxieties inherent in the approach to the dark tower: romance metamorphoses into nursery rhyme to produce the image of the suddenly towering giant, and the knightly child becomes the child indeed, threatened by this terrifying figure. The metamorphosis from Child Rowland to Jack the Giant Killer further defines the source of anxiety: for the world of heroic action is

14Brent Cohen first called my attention to the importance of this song, and particularly of the shift of size implicit within it, for an understanding of Edgar's relationship to his father.

identified in Edgar's mind with the child's attack on the giant, and hence on the father who stands behind the giants of childhood. The aggression of the young man is traced back to its childhood sources; and once this association has been made, the entry into manhood and the realm of heroic action is bound to provoke the retribution of the giant-father. Insofar as Edgar knows that his father wishes to kill him but does not know why, this retribution seems already to have been provoked. In fact, Edgar's tendency to turn punishment against himself may be partly an attempt to placate this monstrous figure; in any event, the apparent retribution of the father is bound to increase the anxiety inherent in action and hence the need for the protection of passivity. It is no wonder that, for this character, to whom action is so momentous and so frightening, ripeness is all.

The role of Poor Tom continues to serve Edgar's needs as long as the knowledge of his father's anger, and hence his own desire for revenge, continue to make action impossible. When Edgar meets his father, penitent and already horribly punished by forces beyond Edgar's control, the needs that dictated the role of Poor Tom begin to disappear. Indeed, Edgar arranges a virtual exorcism for both the desire to punish and the role itself. At Dover Cliff, he participates imaginatively in his father's death in a way that converts potential punishment into cure; this conversion allows him to bid farewell to the concept of his father as fiend, and hence of himself as fiend, that had led them to that cliff. And as the fiends that had haunted Poor Tom disappear, comically exorcised by Edgar's exaggerated description of the fiend accompanying his father, Poor Tom himself disappears; Edgar signals the disappearance of this part of himself by taking on a role that expresses his new sense of himself, especially his newly released capacity for active pity in place of a passive and cowering terror. And when Edgar takes on the role of the most poor man, he celebrates the disappearance of the fiend by calling Gloucester "father" for the first time, though in a generalized phrase that still forestalls recognition (IV. vi. 72). From this moment onward, Edgar's roles move increasingly close to his true identity: for Edgar's disguises throughout are emblematic partly of Edgar's own distance from what he can recognize as himself. As he moves from mad beggar to poor man and peasant, then to armed and nameless noble, and finally to the resumption of his own identity, the progression reflects his increasing integration with his own experience and at the same time, his increasing integration back into the human community.[15] And as he is able to reclaim more of himself, he is able to reclaim more of his father: the movement of his disguises toward self-revelation is paralleled by the movement of his acknowledgement of Gloucester first as Flibbertigibbet, then as "thou happy father" (IV. vi. 72), then simply as "father" (IV. vi. 212; V. ii. 1), and finally as his father indeed.

That we feel Edgar as a force of good, that we hear in his trumpet the echoes of the last judgment, is perfectly consistent with the character we have seen, who must avoid action as an independent agent: Edgar's moral and symbolic meaning grows from the psychological necessities of his character. For Edgar's passive readiness to wait upon the will of the gods, and even his tendency toward a kind of masochism, take on enormous moral force in a world in which nearly everyone else is too ready to act on behalf of self and in which self-serving action and the desire for revenge so often turn toward overt sadism. To suggest that Shakespeare has given us a remarkable portrait of the psychological state underlying Edgar's nobility is in no way an attempt to diminish the moral force of this nobility. Acts of unselfish goodness remain good no matter what their origin; in fact, we may feel their goodness more keenly if we sense in them the successful struggle to overcome the heathland of human impulse terrifyingly released in the role of Poor Tom. Edgar's cure of his father at Dover Cliff is miraculous, no matter how imperfectly achieved, because in it his love for his father triumphs over any remaining anger or desire for revenge; indeed, all the miracles of the play are triumphs of a love that goes beyond cause. The emblems that Edgar creates for us and the philosophic truths to which he gives utterance and in which we want so much to believe are not disembodied entities; and indeed, they would lose much of their force if they were. For we feel them as truths partly insofar as we respond

[15]Edgar's progress is by no means perfect; even at the end, we are likely to be made uncomfortable by his need to disown his own experiences by appealing to the just gods and especially by turning his relationship to his father into a polished narrative (one doubly distasteful because it is superfluous for the audience and because it seems so artificial an imitation of what we have just endured; the phrase "his bleeding rings,/ Their precious stones new lost" [V. iii. 191-92] , for example, robs Gloucester's blinding of precisely that immediacy of experience that makes it unendurable). Nonetheless, the Edgar who at the end recognizes the imperative of speaking what he feels, not what he ought to say, has allowed a larger range of experience to be part of himself than the Edgar who flees into the disguise of Poor Tom; that he does not attempt a moral maxim to ward off the catastrophe he has just seen is one measure of the change in him.

to Edgar openly and as a whole character, acknowledging even those parts of him—and hence of ourselves—that he wishes to disown: insofar, that is, as we respond to him as someone who is not alien to us. And as we respond to Edgar, so must we respond to the whole play: for we as spectators will find this play only insofar as we allow it to find us.

King Lear

by A. C. Bradley

For Dante that which is recorded in the *Divine Comedy* was the justice and love of God. What did *King Lear* record for Shakespeare? Something, it would seem, very different. This is certainly the most terrible picture that Shakespeare painted of the world. In no other of his tragedies does humanity appear more pitiably infirm or more hopelessly bad. What is Iago's malignity against an envied stranger compared with the cruelty of the son of Gloster and the daughters of Lear? What are the sufferings of a strong man like Othello to those of helpless age? Much too that we have already observed — the repetition of the main theme in that of the under-plot, the comparisons of man with the most wretched and the most horrible of the beasts, the impression of Nature's hostility to him, the irony of the unexpected catastrophe — these, with much else, seem even to indicate an intention to show things at their worst, and to return the sternest of replies to that question of the ultimate power and those appeals for retribution. Is it an accident, for example, that Lear's first appeal to something beyond the earth,

> O heavens,
> If you do love old men, if your sweet sway
> Allow obedience, if yourselves are old,
> Make it your cause:

is immediately answered by the iron voices of his daughters, raising by turns the conditions on which they will give him a humiliating harbourage; or that his second appeal, heart-rending in its piteousness,

> You see me here, you gods, a poor old man,
> As full of grief as age; wretched in both:

"King Lear" by A. C. Bradley. From *Shakespearean Tragedy* (London and Basingstoke: Macmillan & Co. Ltd., 1904; New York: St. Martin's Press, Inc., 1957), pp. 273-75, 278-79, 304-305, 315-27. Reprinted by permission of the publishers.

is immediately answered from the heavens by the sound of the breaking storm? Albany and Edgar may moralise on the divine justice as they will, but how, in the face of all that we see, shall we believe that they speak Shakespeare's mind? Is not his mind rather expressed in the bitter contrast between their faith and the events we witness, or in the scornful rebuke of those who take upon them the mystery of things as if they were God's spies? Is it not Shakespeare's judgment on his kind that we hear in Lear's appeal,

> And thou, all-shaking thunder,
> Smite flat the thick rotundity o' the world!
> Crack nature's moulds, all germens spill at once,
> That make ingrateful man!

and Shakespeare's judgment on the worth of existence that we hear in Lear's agonised cry, "No, no, no life!"?

Beyond doubt, I think, some such feelings as these possess us, and, if we follow Shakespeare, ought to possess us, from time to time as we read *King Lear.* And some readers will go further and maintain that this is also the ultimate and total impression left by the tragedy. *King Lear* has been held to be profoundly "pessimistic" in the full meaning of that word,—the record of a time when contempt and loathing for his kind had overmastered the poet's soul, and in despair he pronounced man's life to be simply hateful and hideous. But in fact these descriptions, like most of the remarks made on *King Lear* in the present lecture, emphasise only certain aspects of the play and certain elements in the total impression; and in that impression the effect of these aspects, though far from being lost, is modified by that of others. I do not mean that the final effect resembles that of the *Divine Comedy* or the *Oresteia:* how should it, when the first of these can be called by its author a "Comedy," and when the second, ending (as doubtless the *Prometheus* trilogy also ended) with a solution, is not in the Shakespearean sense a tragedy at all? Nor do I mean that *King Lear* contains a revelation of righteous omnipotence or heavenly harmony, or even a promise of the reconciliation of mystery and justice. But then, as we saw, neither do Shakespeare's other tragedies contain these things. Any theological interpretation of the world on the author's part is excluded from them, and their effect would be disordered or destroyed equally by the ideas of righteous or of unrighteous omnipotence. Nor, in reading them, do we think of "justice" or "equity" in the sense of a strict requital or such an adjustment of merit and prosperity as our moral

sense is said to demand; and there never was vainer labour than that
of critics who try to make out that the persons in these dramas meet
with "justice" or their "deserts." But, on the other hand, man is not
represented in these tragedies as the mere plaything of a blind or
capricious power, suffering woes which have no relation to his character and actions; nor is the world represented as given over to darkness. And in these respects *King Lear,* though the most terrible of
these works, does not differ in essence from the rest. Its keynote is
surely to be heard neither in the words wrung from Gloster in his
anguish,[1] nor in Edgar's words "the gods are just." Its final and
total result is one in which pity and terror, carried perhaps to the
extreme limits of art, are so blended with a sense of law and beauty
that we feel at last, not depression and much less despair, but a consciousness of greatness in pain, and of solemnity in the mystery we
cannot fathom.

There is nothing more noble and beautiful in literature than
Shakespeare's exposition of the effect of suffering in reviving the
greatness and eliciting the sweetness of Lear's nature. The occasional
recurrence, during his madness, of autocratic impatience or of desire
for revenge serves only to heighten this effect, and the moments
when his insanity becomes merely infinitely piteous do not weaken
it. The old King who in pleading with his daughters feels so intensely his own humiliation and their horrible ingratitude, and who yet,
at fourscore and upward, constrains himself to practise a self-control
and patience so many years disused; who out of old affection for his
Fool, and in repentance for his injustice to the Fool's beloved mis-
tress, tolerates incessant and cutting reminders of his own folly and
wrong; in whom the rage of the storm awakes a power and a poetic
grandeur surpassing even that of Othello's anguish; who comes in
his affliction to think of others first, and to seek, in tender solicitude
for his poor boy, the shelter he scorns for his own bare head; who
learns to feel and to pray for the miserable and houseless poor, to
discern the falseness of flattery and the brutality of authority, and to
pierce below the differences of rank and raiment to the common
humanity beneath; whose sight is so purged by scalding tears that it
sees at last how power and place and all things in the world are vanity
except love; who tastes in his last hours the extremes both of love's

[1]["As flies to wanton boys are we to the gods; they kill us for their sport." (IV. i.
36-37)—ed.]

rapture and of its agony,[2] but could never, if he lived on or lived again, care a jot for aught beside—there is no figure, surely, in the world of poetry at once so grand, so pathetic, and so beautiful as his. Well, but Lear owes the whole of this to those sufferings which made us doubt whether life were not simply evil, and men like the flies which wanton boys torture for their sport. Should we not be at least as near the truth if we called this poem *The Redemption of King Lear,* and declared that the business of "the gods" with him was neither to torment him, nor to teach him a "noble anger," but to lead him to attain through apparently hopeless failure the very end and aim of life? One can believe that Shakespeare had been tempted at times to feel misanthropy and despair, but it is quite impossible that he can have been mastered by such feelings at the time when he produced this conception.

There is in the world of *King Lear* the same abundance of extreme good as of extreme evil. It generates in profusion self-less devotion and unconquerable love. And the strange thing is that neither Shakespeare nor we are surprised. We approve these characters, admire them, love them; but we feel no mystery. We do not ask in bewilderment, Is there any cause in nature that makes these kind hearts? Such hardened optimists are we, and Shakespeare,—and those who find the darkness of revelation in a tragedy which reveals Cordelia. Yet surely, if we condemn the universe for Cordelia's death, we ought also to remember that it gave her birth. ...

[2][Later in his essay, Bradley extends this point in a speculation that is the starting point for much later criticism:

Though he is killed by an agony of pain, the agony in which he actually dies is one not of pain but of ecstasy. Suddenly, with a cry represented in the oldest text by a four-times repeated "O," he exclaims:

> Do you see this? Look on her, look, her lips,
> Look there, look there!

These are the last words of Lear. He is sure, at last, that she *lives:* and what had he said when he was still in doubt?

> She lives! if it be so,
> It is a chance which does redeem all sorrows
> That ever I have felt!

To us, perhaps, the knowledge that he is deceived may bring a culmination of pain: but, if it brings *only* that, I believe we are false to Shakespeare, and it seems almost beyond question that any actor is false to the text who does not attempt to express, in Lear's last accents and gestures and look, an unbearable *joy*. — ed.]

The character of Cordelia is not a masterpiece of invention or subtlety like that of Cleopatra; yet in its own way it is a creation as wonderful. Cordelia appears in only four of the twenty-six scenes of *King Lear;* she speaks — it is hard to believe it — scarcely more than a hundred lines; and yet no character in Shakespeare is more absolutely individual or more ineffaceably stamped on the memory of his readers. There is a harmony, strange but perhaps the result of intention, between the character itself and this reserved or parsimonious method of depicting it. An expressiveness almost inexhaustible gained through paucity of expression; the suggestion of infinite wealth and beauty conveyed by the very refusal to reveal this beauty in expansive speech — this is at once the nature of Cordelia herself and the chief characteristic of Shakespeare's art in representing it. Perhaps it is not fanciful to find a parallel in his drawing of a person very different, Hamlet. It was natural to Hamlet to examine himself minutely, to discuss himself at large, and yet to remain a mystery to himself; and Shakespeare's method of drawing the character answers to it; it is extremely detailed and searching, and yet its effect is to enhance the sense of mystery. The results in the two cases differ correspondingly. No one hesitates to enlarge upon Hamlet, who speaks of himself so much; but to use many words about Cordelia seems to be a kind of impiety.

I am obliged to speak of her chiefly because the devotion she inspires almost inevitably obscures her part in the tragedy. This devotion is composed, so to speak, of two contrary elements, reverence and pity. The first, because Cordelia's is a higher nature than that of most even of Shakespeare's heroines. With the tenderness of Viola or Desdemona she unites something of the resolution, power, and dignity of Hermione, and reminds us sometimes of Helena, sometimes of Isabella, though she has none of the traits which prevent Isabella from winning our hearts. Her assertion of truth and right, her allegiance to them, even the touch of severity that accompanies it, instead of compelling mere respect or admiration, become adorable in a nature so loving as Cordelia's. She is a thing enskyed and sainted, and yet we feel no incongruity in the love of the King of France for her, as we do in the love of the Duke for Isabella.

But with this reverence or worship is combined in the reader's mind a passion of championship, of pity, even of protecting pity. She is so deeply wronged, and she appears, for all her strength, so defenceless. We think of her as unable to speak for herself. We think of her as quite young, and as slight and small. "Her voice was ever soft, gentle, and low"; ever so, whether the tone was that of resolution, or rebuke, or love. Of all Shakespeare's heroines she knew least of joy. She grew up with Goneril and Regan for sisters. Even her love for her father must have been mingled with pain and anxiety. She must early have learned to school and repress emotion. She never knew the bliss of young love: there is no trace of such love for the King of France. She had knowingly to wound most deeply the being dearest to her. He cast her off; and, after suffering an agony for him, and before she could see him safe in death, she was brutally murdered. We have to thank the poet for passing lightly over the circumstances of her death. We do not think of them. Her image comes before us calm and bright and still.

The memory of Cordelia thus becomes detached in a manner from the action of the drama. The reader refuses to admit into it any idea of imperfection, and is outraged when any share in her father's sufferings is attributed to the part she plays in the opening scene. Because she was deeply wronged he is ready to insist that she was wholly right. He refuses, that is, to take the tragic point of view, and, when it is taken, he imagines that Cordelia is being attacked, or is being declared to have "deserved" all that befell her. But Shakespeare's was the tragic point of view. He exhibits in the opening scene a situation tragic for Cordelia as well as for Lear. At a moment where terrible issues join, Fate makes on her the one demand which she is unable to meet. As I have already remarked in speaking of Desdemona, it was a demand which other heroines of Shakespeare could have met. Without loss of self-respect, and refusing even to appear to compete for a reward, they could have made the unreasonable old King feel that he was fondly loved. Cordelia cannot, because she is Cordelia. And so she is not merely rejected and banished, but her father is left to the mercies of her sisters. And the cause of her failure — a failure a thousand-fold redeemed — is a compound in which imperfection appears so intimately mingled with the noblest qualities that — if we are true to Shakespeare — we do not think either of justifying her or of blaming her: we feel simply the tragic emotions of fear and pity.

In this failure a large part is played by that obvious characteristic to which I have already referred. Cordelia is not, indeed, always tongue-tied, as several passages in the drama, and even in this scene, clearly show. But tender emotion, and especially a tender love for the person to whom she has to speak, makes her dumb. Her love, as she says, is more ponderous than her tongue:

> Unhappy that I am, I cannot heave
> My heart into my mouth.

This expressive word "heave" is repeated in the passage which describes her reception of Kent's letter:

> Faith, once or twice she heaved the name of "Father"
> Pantingly forth, as if it press'd her heart:

two or three broken ejaculations escape her lips, and she "starts" away "to deal with grief alone." The same trait reappears with an ineffable beauty in the stifled repetitions with which she attempts to answer her father in the moment of his restoration:

> *Lear.*   Do not laugh at me;
> For, as I am a man, I think this lady
> To be my child Cordelia.
> *Cor.*   And so I am, I am.
> *Lear.* Be your tears wet? yes, faith. I pray, weep not;
> If you have poison for me, I will drink it.
> I know you do not love me; for your sisters
> Have, as I do remember, done me wrong:
> You have some cause, they have not.
> *Cor.*   No cause, no cause.

We see this trait for the last time, marked by Shakespeare with a decision clearly intentional, in her inability to answer one syllable to the last words we hear her father speak to her:

> No, no, no, no! Come, let's away to prison:
> We two alone will sing like birds i' the cage:
> When thou dost ask me blessing, I'll kneel down,
> And ask of thee forgiveness: so we'll live,
> And pray, and sing, and tell old tales, and laugh
> At gilded butterflies. . . .

She stands and weeps, and goes out with him silent. And we see her alive no more.

But (I am forced to dwell on the point, because I am sure to slur it over is to be false to Shakespeare) this dumbness of love was not the sole source of misunderstanding. If this had been all, even Lear could have seen the love in Cordelia's eyes when, to his question "What can you say to draw a third more opulent than your sisters?" she answered "Nothing." But it did not shine there. She is not merely silent, nor does she merely answer "Nothing." She tells him that she loves him "according to her bond, nor more nor less"; and his answer,

> How now, Cordelia! mend your speech a little,
> Lest it may mar your fortunes.

so intensifies her horror at the hypocrisy of her sisters that she replies,

> Good my lord,
> You have begot me, bred me, loved me: I
> Return those duties back as are right fit,
> Obey you, love you, and most honour you.
> Why have my sisters husbands, if they say
> They love you all? Haply, when I shall wed,
> That lord whose hand must take my plight shall carry
> Half my love with him, half my care and duty:
> Sure, I shall never marry like my sisters,
> To love my father all.

What words for the ear of an old father, unreasonable, despotic, but fondly loving, indecent in his own expressions of preference, and blind to the indecency of his appeal for protestations of fondness! Blank astonishment, anger, wounded love, contend within him; but for the moment he restrains himself and asks,

> But goes thy heart with this?

Imagine Imogen's reply! But Cordelia answers,

> Ay, good my lord.
> *Lear.* So young, and so untender?
> *Cor.* So young, my lord, and true.

Yes, "heavenly true." But truth is not the only good in the world, nor is the obligation to tell truth the only obligation. The matter here was to keep it inviolate, but also to preserve a father. And even if truth *were* the one and only obligation, to tell much less than truth is not to tell it. And Cordelia's speech not only tells much less than truth about her love, it actually perverts the truth when it implies that to give love to a husband is to take it from a father. There surely never was a more unhappy speech.

When Isabella goes to plead with Angelo for her brother's life, her horror of her brother's sin is so intense, and her perception of the justice of Angelo's reasons for refusing her is so clear and keen, that she is ready to abandon her appeal before it is well begun; she would actually do so but that the warm-hearted profligate Lucio reproaches her for her coldness and urges her on. Cordelia's hatred of hypocrisy and of the faintest appearance of mercenary professions reminds us of Isabella's hatred of impurity; but Cordelia's position is infinitely more difficult, and on the other hand there is mingled with her hatred a touch of personal antagonism and of pride. Lear's words,

> Let pride, which she calls plainness, marry her!

are monstrously unjust, but they contain one grain of truth; and indeed it was scarcely possible that a nature so strong as Cordelia's, and with so keen a sense of dignity, should feel here nothing whatever of pride and resentment. This side of her character is emphatically shown in her language to her sisters in the first scene — language perfectly just, but little adapted to soften their hearts towards their father — and again in the very last words we hear her speak. She and her father are brought in, prisoners, to the enemy's camp; but she sees only Edmund, not those "greater" ones on whose pleasure hangs her father's fate and her own. For her own she is little concerned; she knows how to meet adversity:

> For thee, oppressed king, am I cast down;
> Myself could else out-frown false fortune's frown.

Yes, that is how she would meet fortune, frowning it down, even as Goneril would have met it; nor, if her father had been already dead, would there have been any great improbability in the false story that was to be told of her death, that, like Goneril, she "fordid herself." Then, after those austere words about fortune, she suddenly asks,

> Shall we not see these daughters and these sisters?

Strange last words for us to hear from a being so worshipped and beloved; but how characteristic! Their tone is unmistakable. I doubt if she could have brought herself to plead with her sisters for her father's life; and if she had attempted the task, she would have performed it but ill. Nor is our feeling towards her altered one whit by that. But what is true of Kent and the Fool is, in its measure, true of her. Any one of them would gladly have died a hundred deaths to help King Lear; and they do help his soul; but they harm his cause. They are all involved in tragedy.

Why does Cordelia die? I suppose no reader ever failed to ask that question, and to ask it with something more than pain,—to ask it, if only for a moment, in bewilderment or dismay, and even perhaps in tones of protest. These feelings are probably evoked more strongly here than at the death of any other notable character in Shakespeare; and it may sound a wilful paradox to assert that the slightest element of reconciliation is mingled with them or succeeds them. Yet it seems to me indubitable that such an element is present, though difficult to make out with certainty what it is or whence it proceeds. And I will try to make this out, and to state it methodically.

(a) It is not due in any perceptible degree to the fact, which we have just been examining, that Cordelia through her tragic imperfection contributes something to the conflict and catastrophe; and I drew attention to that imperfection without any view to our present problem. The critics who emphasise it at this point in the drama are surely untrue to Shakespeare's mind; and still more completely astray are those who lay stress on the idea that Cordelia in bringing a foreign army to help her father was guilty of treason to her country. When she dies we regard her, practically speaking, simply as we regard Ophelia or Desdemona, as an innocent victim swept away in the convulsion caused by the error or guilt of others.

(b) Now this destruction of the good through the evil of others is one of the tragic facts of life, and no one can object to the use of it, within certain limits, in tragic art. And, further, those who because of it declaim against the nature of things, declaim without thinking. It is obviously the other side of the fact that the effects of good spread far and wide beyond the doer of good; and we should ask ourselves whether we really could wish (supposing it conceivable) to see this double-sided fact abolished. Nevertheless the touch of reconciliation that we feel in contemplating the death of Cordelia is not due, or is due only in some slight degree, to a perception that the event is true to life, admissible in tragedy, and a case of a law which we cannot seriously desire to see abrogated.

(c) What then is this feeling, and whence does it come? I believe that we shall find that it is a feeling not confined to *King Lear,* but present at the close of other tragedies; and that the reason why it has an exceptional tone or force at the close of *King Lear,* lies in that very peculiarity of the close which also—at least for the moment— excites bewilderment, dismay, or protest. The feeling I mean is the impression that the heroic being, though in one sense and outward-

ly he has failed, is yet in another sense superior to the world in which he appears; is, in some way which we do not seek to define, untouched by the doom that overtakes him; and is rather set free from life than deprived of it. Some such feeling as this—some feeling which, from this description of it, may be recognised as their own even by those who would dissent from the description—we surely have in various degrees at the deaths of Hamlet and Othello and Lear, and of Antony and Cleopatra and Coriolanus. It accompanies the more prominent tragic impressions, and, regarded alone, could hardly be called tragic. For it seems to imply (though we are probably quite unconscious of the implication) an idea which, if developed, would transform the tragic view of things. It implies that the tragic world, if taken as it is presented, with all its error, guilt, failure, woe and waste, is no final reality, but only a part of reality taken for the whole, and, when so taken, illusive; and that if we could see the whole, and the tragic facts in their true place in it, we should find them, not abolished, of course, but so transmuted that they had ceased to be strictly tragic,—find, perhaps, the suffering and death counting for little or nothing, the greatness of the soul for much or all, and the heroic spirit, in spite of failure, nearer to the heart of things than the smaller, more circumspect, and perhaps even "better" beings who survived the catastrophe. The feeling which I have tried to describe, as accompanying the more obvious tragic emotions at the deaths of heroes, corresponds with some such idea as this.

Now this feeling is evoked with a quite exceptional strength by the death of Cordelia. It is not due to the perception that she, like Lear, has attained through suffering; we know that she had suffered and attained in his days of prosperity. It is simply the feeling that what happens to such a being does not matter; all that matters is what she is. How this can be when, for anything the tragedy tells us, she has ceased to exist, we do not ask; but the tragedy itself makes us feel that somehow it is so. And the force with which this impression is conveyed depends largely on· the very fact which excites our bewilderment and protest, that her death, following on the deaths of all the evil characters, and brought about by an unexplained delay in Edmund's effort to save her, comes on us, not as an inevitable conclusion to the sequence of events, but as the sudden stroke of mere fate or chance. The force of the impression, that is to say, depends on the very violence of the contrast between the outward and the inward, Cordelia's death and Cordelia's soul. The more unmotived, unmerited, senseless, monstrous, her fate, the more do we feel that it does not concern her. The extremity of the disproportion between prosperity and goodness first shocks us, and then flashes on us the conviction that our whole attitude in asking or expecting that goodness should be prosperous is wrong; that, if only we could see things as they are, we should see that the outward is nothing and the inward is all.

And some such thought as this (which, to bring it clearly out, I have stated, and still state, in a form both exaggerated and much too explicit) is really present through the whole play. Whether Shakespeare knew it or not, it is present. I might almost say that the "moral" of *King Lear* is presented in the irony of this collocation:

> *Albany.* The gods defend her!
> *(Enter Lear with Cordelia dead in his arms.)*

The "gods," it seems, do *not* show their approval by "defending" their own from adversity or death, or by giving them power and prosperity. These, on the contrary, are worthless, or worse; it is not on them, but on the renunciation of them, that the gods throw incense. They breed lust, pride, hardness of heart, the insolence of office, cruelty, scorn, hypocrisy, contention, war, murder, self-destruction. The whole story beats this indictment of prosperity into the brain. Lear's great speeches in his madness proclaim it like the curses of Timon on life and man. But here, as in *Timon,* the poor and humble are, almost without exception, sound and sweet at heart, faithful and pitiful. And here adversity, to the blessed in spirit, is blessed. It wins fragrance from the crushed flower. It melts in aged hearts sympathies which prosperity had frozen. It purges the soul's sight by blinding that of the eyes. Throughout that stupendous Third Act the good are seen growing better through suffering, and the bad worse through success. The warm castle is a room in hell, the storm-swept heath a sanctuary. The judgment of this world is a lie; its goods, which we covet, corrupt us; its ills, which break our bodies, set our souls free;

> Our means secure us, and our mere defects
> Prove our commodities.

Let us renounce the world, hate it, and lose it gladly. The only real thing in it is the soul, with its courage, patience, devotion. And nothing outward can touch that.

King Lear and the Comedy of
the Grotesque

by G. Wilson Knight

It may appear strange to search for any sort of comedy as a primary theme in a play whose abiding gloom is so heavy, whose reading of human destiny and human actions so starkly tragic. Yet it is an error of aesthetic judgement to regard humour as essentially trivial. Though its impact usually appears vastly different from that of tragedy, yet there is a humour that treads the brink of tears, and tragedy which needs but an infinitesimal shift of perspective to disclose the varied riches of comedy. Humour is an evanescent thing, even more difficult of analysis and intellectual location than tragedy. To the coarse mind lacking sympathy an incident may seem comic which to the richer understanding is pitiful and tragic. So, too, one series of facts can be treated by the artist as either comic or tragic, lending itself equivalently to both. Sometimes a great artist may achieve significant effects by a criss-cross of tears and laughter. Tchehov does this, especially in his plays. A shifting flash of comedy across the pain of the purely tragic both increases the tension and suggests, vaguely, a resolution and a purification. The comic and the tragic rest both on the idea of incompatibilities, and are also, themselves, mutually exclusive: therefore to mingle them is to add to the meaning of each; for the result is then but a new sublime incongruity.

King Lear is roughly analogous to Tchehov where *Macbeth* is analogous to Dostoievsky. The wonder of Shakespearian tragedy is ever a mystery—a vague, yet powerful, tangible, presence; an interlocking of the mind with a profound meaning, a disclosure to the inward eye of vistas undreamed, and but fitfully understood. *King*

"*King Lear* and the Comedy of the Grotesque" by G. Wilson Knight. From *The Wheel of Fire* (London: Methuen & Co. Ltd., 1949), pp. 160-76, 4th edition revised. Copyright 1949 by Methuen & Co. Ltd. Reprinted by permission of the publisher.

Lear is great in the abundance and richness of human delineation, in the level focus of creation that builds a massive oneness, in fact, a universe, of single quality from a multiplicity of differentiated units; and in a positive and purposeful working out of a purgatorial philosophy. But it is still greater in the perfect fusion of psychological realism with the daring flights of a fantastic imagination. The heart of a Shakespearian tragedy is centred in the imaginative, in the unknown; and in *King Lear,* where we touch the unknown, we touch the fantastic. The peculiar dualism at the root of this play which wrenches and splits the mind by a sight of incongruities displays in turn realities absurd, hideous, pitiful. This incongruity is Lear's madness; it is also the demonic laughter that echoes in the *Lear* universe. In pure tragedy the dualism of experience is continually being dissolved in the masterful beauty of passion, merged in the sunset of emotion. But in comedy it is not so softly resolved —incompatibilities stand out till the sudden relief of laughter or its equivalent of humour: therefore incongruity is the especial mark of comedy. Now in *King Lear* there is a dualism continually crying in vain to be resolved either by tragedy or comedy. Thence arises its peculiar tension of pain: and the course of the action often comes as near to the resolution of comedy as to that of tragedy. So I shall notice here the imaginative core of the play, and, excluding much of the logic of the plot from immediate attention, analyse the fantastic comedy of *King Lear.*

From the start, the situation has a comic aspect. It has been observed that Lear has, so to speak, staged an interlude, with himself as chief actor, in which he grasps expressions of love to his heart, and resigns his sceptre to a chorus of acclamations. It is childish, foolish—but very human. So, too, is the result. Sincerity forbids play-acting, and Cordelia cannot subdue her instinct to any judgement advising tact rather than truth. The incident is profoundly comic and profoundly pathetic. It is, indeed, curious that so storm-furious a play as *King Lear* should have so trivial a domestic basis: it is the first of our many incongruities to be noticed. The absurdity of the old King's anger is clearly indicated by Kent:

> Kill thy physician, and the fee bestow
> Upon the foul disease.   (I. i. 166)

The result is absurd. Lear's loving daughter Cordelia is struck from his heart's register, and he is shortly, old and grey-haired and a king, cutting a cruelly ridiculous figure before the cold sanity of

his unloving elder daughters. Lear is selfish, self-centred. The
images he creates of his three daughters' love are quite false, sen-
timentalized: he understands the nature of none of his children, and
demanding an unreal and impossible love from all three, is dis-
illusioned by each in turn. But, though sentimental, this love is not
weak. It is powerful and firm-planted in his mind as a mountain
rock embedded in earth. The tearing out of it is hideous, cataclysmic.
A tremendous soul is, as it were, incongruously geared to a puerile
intellect. Lear's senses prove his idealized love-figments false, his
intellect snaps, and, as the loosened drive flings limp, the discon-
nected engine of madness spins free, and the ungeared revolutions
of it are terrible, fantastic. This, then, is the basis of the play: greatness linked to puerility. Lear's instincts are themselves grand,
heroic — noble even. His judgement is nothing. He understands
neither himself nor his daughters:

> Regan. 'Tis the infirmity of his age: yet he hath ever but slenderly
> known himself.
> Goneril. The best and soundest of his time hath been but rash...
>   (I. i. 296)

Lear starts his own tragedy by a foolish misjudgement. Lear's fault
is a fault of the mind, a mind unwarrantably, because selfishly,
foolish. And he knows it:

> O Lear, Lear, Lear!
> Beat at this gate that let thy folly in,
> And thy dear judgement out!   (I. iv. 294)

His purgatory is to be a purgatory of the mind, of madness. Lear has
trained himself to think he cannot be wrong: he finds he is wrong.
He has fed his heart on sentimental knowledge of his children's
love: he finds their love is not sentimental. There is now a gaping
dualism in his mind, thus drawn asunder by incongruities, and he
endures madness. Thus the theme of the play is bodied continually
into a fantastic incongruity, which is implicit in the beginning — in
the very act of Lear's renunciation, retaining the "title and addition"
of King, yet giving over a king's authority to his children. As he becomes torturingly aware of the truth, incongruity masters his mind,
and fantastic madness ensues; and this peculiar fact of the Lear-
theme is reflected in the *Lear* universe:

> Gloucester. These late eclipses in the sun and moon portend no
> good to us: though the wisdom of nature can reason it thus and

> thus, yet nature finds itself scourged by the sequent effects: love
> cools, friendship falls off, brothers divide: in cities, mutinies; in
> countries, discord; in palaces, treason; and the bond cracked 'twixt
> son and father. This villain of mine comes under the prediction;
> there's son against father: the King falls from bias of nature;
> there's father gainst child. We have seen the best of our time:
> machinations, hollowness, treachery, and all ruinous disorders,
> follow us disquietly to our graves.   (i. ii. 115)

Gloucester's words hint a universal incongruity here: the fantastic
incongruity of parent and child opposed. And it will be most helpful
later to notice the Gloucester-theme in relation to that of Lear.

From the first signs of Goneril's cruelty, the Fool is used as a
chorus, pointing us to the absurdity of the situation. He is indeed an
admirable chorus, increasing our pain by his emphasis on a humour
which yet will not serve to merge the incompatible in a unity of
laughter. He is not all wrong when he treats the situation as matter for a joke. Much here that is always regarded as essentially pathetic is not far from comedy. For instance, consider Lear's words:

> I will have such revenges on you both
> That all the world shall — I will do such things —
> What they are, yet I know not; but they shall be
> The terrors of the earth.   (II. iv. 282)

What could be more painfully incongruous, spoken, as it is, by an
old man, a king, to his daughter? It is not far from the ridiculous.
The very thought seems a sacrilegious cruelty, I know: but ridicule
is generally cruel. The speeches of Lear often come near comedy.
Again, notice the abrupt contrast in his words:

> But yet thou art my flesh, my blood, my daughter;
> Or rather a disease that's in my flesh,
> Which I must needs call mine: thou art a boil,
> A plague-sore, an embossed carbuncle,
> In my corrupted blood. But I'll not chide thee...
>
> (II. iv. 224)

This is not comedy, nor humour. But it is exactly the stuff of which
humour is made. Lear is mentally a child; in passion a titan. The
absurdity of his every act at the beginning of his tragedy is contrasted with the dynamic fury which intermittently bursts out,
flickers — then flames and finally gives us those grand apostrophes
lifted from man's stage of earth to heaven's rain and fire and thunder:

> Blow, winds, and crack your cheeks! rage! blow!
> You cataracts and hurricanoes, spout
> Till you have drench'd our steeples, drown'd the cocks!
>
> (III. ii. 1)

Two speeches of this passionate and unrestrained volume of Promethean curses are followed by:

> No, I will be the pattern of all patience;
> I will say nothing.   (III. ii. 37)

Again we are in touch with potential comedy: a slight shift of perspective, and the incident is rich with humour. A sense of self-directed humour would, indeed, have saved Lear. It is a quality he absolutely lacks.

Herein lies the profound insight of the Fool: he sees the potentialities of comedy in Lear's behaviour. This old man, recently a king, and, if his speeches are fair samples, more than a little of a tyrant, now goes from daughter to daughter, furious because Goneril dares criticize his pet knights, kneeling down before Regan, performing, as she says, "unsightly tricks" (II. iv. 159)—the situation is excruciatingly painful, and its painfulness is exactly of that quality which embarrasses in some forms of comedy. In the theatre, one is terrified lest some one laugh: yet, if Lear could laugh—if the Lears of the world could laugh at themselves—there would be no such tragedy. In the early scenes old age and dignity suffer, and seem to deserve, the punishments of childhood:

> Now, by my life,
> Old fools are babes again; and must be used
> With checks as flatteries.   (I. iii. 19)

The situation is summed up by the Fool:

> *Lear.* When were you wont to be so full of songs, sirrah?
> *Fool.* I have used it, nuncle, ever since thou madest thy daughters
>   thy mother: for when thou gavest them the rod, and put'st down
>   thine own breeches.... (I. iv. 186)

The height of indecency in suggestion, the height of incongruity. Lear is spiritually put to the ludicrous shame endured bodily by Kent in the stocks: and the absurd rant of Kent, and the unreasonable childish temper of Lear, both merit in some measure what they receive. Painful as it may sound, that is, provisionally, a truth we should realize. The Fool realizes it. He is, too, necessary. Here,

where the plot turns on the diverging tugs of two assurances in the
mind, it is natural that the action be accompanied by some symbol
of humour, that mode which is built of unresolved incompatibilities.
Lear's torment is a torment of this dualistic kind, since he scarcely
believes his senses when his daughters resist him. He repeats the
history of Troilus, who cannot understand the faithlessness of Cres-
sid. In *Othello* and *Timon of Athens* the transition is swift from extreme love to revenge or hate. The movement of Lear's mind is less
direct: like Troilus, he is suspended between two separate assurances. Therefore Pandarus, in the latter acts of *Troilus and Cressida,* plays a part similar to the Fool in *King Lear:* both attempt to
heal the gaping wound of the mind's incongruous knowledge by the
unifying, healing release of laughter. They make no attempt to di-
vert, but rather to direct the hero's mind to the present incongruity.
The Fool sees, or tries to see, the humorous potentialities in the most
heart-wrenching of incidents:

> *Lear.* O me, my heart, my rising heart! but, down!
> *Fool.* Cry to it, nuncle, as the cockney did to the eels when she put
> 'em i' the paste alive; she knapped 'em o' the coxcombs with a
> stick, and cried "Down, wantons, down!" 'Twas her brother that,
> in pure kindness to his horse, buttered his hay. (II. iv. 122)

Except for the last delightful touch—the antithesis of the other—
that is a cruel, ugly sense of humour. It is the sinister humour at
the heart of this play: we are continually aware of the humour of
cruelty and the cruelty of humour. But the Fool's use of it is not
aimless. If Lear could laugh he might yet save his reason.

But there is no relief. Outside, in the wild country, the storm
grows more terrible:

> *Kent.*   ...Since I was man
> Such sheets of fire, such bursts of horrid thunder,
> Such groans of roaring wind and rain, I never
> Remember to have heard... (III. ii. 45)

Lear's mind keeps returning to the unreality, the impossibility of
what has happened:

> Your old kind father, whose frank heart gave all—
> O, that way madness lies; let me shun that;
> No more of that. (III. iv. 20)

He is still self-centred; cannot understand that he has been any-

thing but a perfect father; cannot understand his daughters' behaviour. It is

> as this mouth should tear this hand
> For lifting food to't...   (III. iv. 15)

It is incongruous, impossible. There is no longer any "rule in unity
itself."[1] Just as Lear's mind begins to fail, the Fool finds Edgar
disguised as "poor Tom." Edgar now succeeds the Fool as the coun-
terpart to the breaking sanity of Lear; and where the humour of the
Fool made no contact with Lear's mind, the fantastic appearance and
incoherent words of Edgar are immediately assimilated, as glasses
correctly focused to the sight of oncoming madness. Edgar turns the
balance of Lear's wavering mentality. His fantastic appearance and
lunatic irrelevancies, with the storm outside, and the Fool still for
occasional chorus, create a scene of wraithlike unreason, a vision of
a world gone mad:

> ...Bless thy five wits! Tom's a-cold—O, do de, do de, do de. Bless
> thee from whirlwinds, star-blasting, and taking! Do poor Tom some
> charity, whom the foul fiend vexes: there could I have him now—and
> there—and there again, and there.   (III. iv. 57)

To Lear his words are easily explained. His daughters "have brought
him to this pass." He cries:

> *Lear.* Is it the fashion that discarded fathers
>   Should have thus little mercy on their flesh?
>   Judicious punishment! 'twas this flesh begot
>   Those pelican daughters.
> *Edgar.* Pillicock sat on Pillicock-hill:
>   Halloo, halloo, loo, loo!
> *Fool.* This cold night will turn us all to fools and madmen.
>   (III. iv. 71)

What shall we say of this exquisite movement? Is it comedy? Lear's
profound unreason is capped by the blatant irrelevance of Edgar's
couplet suggested by the word "pelican"; then the two are swiftly
all but unified, for us if not for Lear, in the healing balm of the
Fool's conclusion. It is the process of humour, where two incompati-
bles are resolved in laughter. The Fool does this again. Lear again
speaks a profound truth as the wild night and Edgar's fantastic im-
personation grip his mind and dethrone his conventional sanity:

[1] *Troilus and Cressida*, V. ii. 138.

> *Lear.* Is man no more than this? Consider him well. Thou owest
> the worm no silk, the beast no hide, the sheep no wool, the cat
> no perfume. Ha! Here's three on 's are sophisticated! Thou art
> the thing itself: unaccommodated man is no more but such a
> poor, bare, forked animal as thou art. Off, off, you lendings!
> come unbutton here. *(Tearing off his clothes.)*
> *Fool.* Prithee, nuncle, be contented; 'tis a naughty night to swim in.
> (III. iv. 105)

This is the furthest flight, not of tragedy, but of philosophic comedy.
The autocratic and fiery-fierce old king, symbol of dignity, is confronted with the meanest of men: a naked lunatic beggar. In a flash
of vision he attempts to become his opposite, to be naked, "un-
sophisticated." And then the opposing forces which struck the light-
ning-flash of vision tail off, resolved into a perfect unity by the
Fool's laughter, reverberating, trickling, potent to heal in sanity
the hideous unreason of this tempest-shaken night: "'tis a naughty
night to swim in." Again this is the process of humour: its flash of
vision first bridges the positive and negative poles of the mind, unifying them, and then expresses itself in laughter.

This scene grows still more grotesque, fantastical, sinister. Gloucester enters, his torch flickering in the beating wind:

> *Fool.* ...Look, here comes a walking fire.
> *(Enter* Gloucester, *with a torch.)*
> *Edgar.* This is the foul fiend Flibbertigibbet: he begins at curfew
> and walks till the first cock...   (III. iv. 116)

Lear welcomes Edgar as his "philosopher," since he embodies that
philosophy of incongruity and the fantastically-absurd which is
Lear's vision in madness. "Noble philosopher," he says (III. iv. 176),
and "I will still keep with my philosopher" (III. iv. 180). The unresolved dualism that tormented Troilus and was given metaphysical expression by him (*Troilus and Cressida,* V. ii. 134-57) is here
more perfectly bodied into the poetic symbol of poor Tom: and since
Lear cannot hear the resolving laugh of foolery, his mind is focused
only to the "philosopher" mumbling of the foul fiend. Edgar thus
serves to lure Lear on: we forget that he is dissimulating. Lear is the
centre of our attention, and as the world shakes with tempest and unreason, we endure something of the shaking and the tempest of his
mind. The absurd and fantastic reign supreme. Lear does not compass for more than a few speeches the "noble anger" (II. iv. 279) for
which he prayed, the anger of Timon. From the start he wavered

between affection and disillusionment, love and hate. The heavens
in truth "fool" (II. iv. 278) him. He is the "natural fool of fortune"
(IV. vi. 196). Now his anger begins to be a lunatic thing, and when
it rises to any sort of magnificent fury or power it is toppled over by
the ridiculous capping of Edgar's irrelevancies:

> *Lear.* To have a thousand with red burning spits
>   Come hissing in upon 'em —
> *Edgar.* The foul fiend bites my back.   (III. vi. 17)

The mock trial is instituted. Lear's curses were for a short space
terrible, majestic, less controlled and purposeful than Timon's but
passionate and grand in their tempestuous fury. Now, in madness,
he flashes on us the ridiculous basis of his tragedy in words which
emphasize the indignity and incongruity of it, and make his madness something nearer the ridiculous than the terrible, something
which moves our pity, but does not strike awe:

> Arraign her first; 'tis Goneril. I here take my oath before this honour-
> able assembly, she kicked the poor king her father.   (III. vi. 49)

This stroke of the absurd — so vastly different from the awe we
experience in face of Timon's hate — is yet fundamental here. The
core of the play is an absurdity, an indignity, an incongruity. In no
tragedy of Shakespeare does incident and dialogue so recklessly
and miraculously walk the tight-rope of our pity over the depths
of bathos and absurdity.

This particular region of the terrible bordering on the fantastic
and absurd is exactly the playground of madness. Thus the setting
of Lear's madness includes a sub-plot where these same elements
are presented with stark nakedness, and no veiling subtleties. The
Gloucester-theme is a certain indication of our vision and helps us
to understand, and feel, the enduring agony of Lear. As usual, the
first scene of this play strikes the dominant note. Gloucester jests at
the bastardy of his son Edmund, remarking that, though he is
ashamed to acknowledge him, "there was good sport at his making"
(I. i. 23). That is, we start with humour in bad taste. The whole
tragedy witnesses a sense of humour in "the gods" which is in similar
bad taste. Now all the Lear effects are exaggerated in the Gloucester
theme. Edmund's plot is a more Iago-like, devilish, intentional
thing than Goneril's and Regan's icy callousness. Edgar's supposed
letter is crude and absurd:

...I begin to find an idle and fond bondage in the oppression of aged
tyranny... (I. ii. 53)

But then Edmund, wittiest and most attractive of villains, composed
it. One can almost picture his grin as he penned those lines, com-
mending them mentally to the limited intellect of his father. Yes—
the Gloucester theme has a beginning even more fantastic than that
of Lear's tragedy. And not only are the Lear effects here exaggerated
in the directions of villainy and humour: they are even more clearly
exaggerated in that of horror. The gouging out of Gloucester's eyes
is a thing unnecessary, crude, disgusting: it is meant to be. It helps
to provide an accompanying exaggeration of one element—that of
cruelty—in the horror that makes Lear's madness. And not only
horror: there is even again something satanically comic bedded
deep in it. The sight of physical torment, to the uneducated, brings
laughter. Shakespeare's England delighted in watching both physical torment and the comic ravings of actual lunacy. The dance of
madmen in Webster's *Duchess of Malfi* is of the same ghoulish humour as Regan's plucking Gloucester by the beard: the groundlings
will laugh at both. Moreover, the sacrilege of the human body in
torture must be, to a human mind, incongruous, absurd. This
hideous mockery is consummated in Regan's final witticism after
Gloucester's eyes are out:

> Go, thrust him out at gates, and let him smell
> His way to Dover. (III. vii. 93)

The macabre humoresque of this is nauseating: but it is there, and
integral to the play. These ghoulish horrors, so popular in Elizabethan drama, and the very stuff of the *Lear* of Shakespeare's youth,
Titus Andronicus, find an exquisitely appropriate place in the
tragedy of Shakespeare's maturity which takes as its especial prov-
ince this territory of the grotesque and the fantastic which is Lear's
madness. We are clearly pointed to this grim fun, this hideous sense
of humour, at the back of tragedy:

> As flies to wanton boys are we to the gods;
> They kill us for their sport. (IV. i. 36)

This illustrates the exact quality I wish to emphasize: the humour
a boy—even a kind boy—may see in the wriggles of an impaled in-
sect. So, too, Gloucester is bound, and tortured, physically; and so

the mind of Lear is impaled, crucified on the cross-beams of love and
disillusion.

There follows the grim pilgrimage of Edgar and Gloucester towards Dover Cliff: an incident typical enough of *King Lear*—

> 'Tis the times' plague when madmen lead the blind.
>
> (IV. i. 46)

They stumble on, madman and blind man, Edgar mumbling:

> ...five fiends have been in poor Tom at once; of lust, as Obidicut;
> Hobbididance, prince of dumbness; Mahu, of stealing; Modo, of
> murder; Flibbertigibbet, of mopping and mowing, who since pos-
> sesses chambermaids and waiting-women...   (IV. i. 59)

They are near Dover. Edgar persuades his father that they are climb-
ing steep ground, though they are on a level field, that the sea can be
heard beneath:

> *Gloucester.* Methinks the ground is even.
> *Edgar.*   Horrible steep.
>   Hark, do you hear the sea?
> *Gloucester.*   No, truly.
> *Edgar.* Why, then your other senses grow imperfect
>   By your eyes' anguish.
>
> (IV. vi. 3)

Gloucester notices the changed sanity of Edgar's speech, and remarks thereon. Edgar hurries his father to the supposed brink, and
vividly describes the dizzy precipice over which Gloucester thinks
they stand:

> How fearful
> And dizzy 'tis to cast one's eyes so low!
> The crows and choughs that wing the midway air
> Show scarce so gross as beetles: half way down
> Hangs one that gathers samphire, dreadful trade!...
>
> (IV. vi. 12)

Gloucester thanks him, and rewards him; bids him move off; then
kneels, and speaks a prayer of noble resignation, breathing that
stoicism which permeates the suffering philosophy of this play:

> O you mighty gods!
> This world I do renounce, and, in your sights,
> Shake patiently my great affliction off:
> If I could bear it longer, and not fall
> To quarrel with your great opposeless wills,

> My snuff and loathed part of nature should
> Burn itself out.   (IV. vi. 35)

Gloucester has planned a spectacular end for himself. We are given these noble descriptive and philosophical speeches to tune our minds to a noble, tragic sacrifice. And what happens? The old man falls from his kneeling posture a few inches, flat, face foremost. Instead of the dizzy circling to crash and spill his life on the rocks below—just this. The grotesque merged into the ridiculous reaches a consummation in this bathos of tragedy: it is the furthest, most exaggerated, reach of the poet's towering fantastically. We have a sublimely daring stroke of technique, unjustifiable, like Edgar's emphasized and vigorous madness throughout, on the plane of plot-logic, and even to a superficial view somewhat out of place imaginatively in so dire and stark a limning of human destiny as is *King Lear;* yet this scene is in reality a consummate stroke of art. The Gloucester-theme throughout reflects and emphasizes and exaggerates all the percurrent qualities of the Lear-theme. Here the incongruous and fantastic element of the Lear-theme is boldly reflected into the tragically-absurd. The stroke is audacious, unashamed, and magical of effect. Edgar keeps up the deceit; persuades his father that he has really fallen; points to the empty sky, as to a cliff:

> ...the shrill-gorged lark
> Cannot be heard so far...   (IV. vi. 59)

and finally paints a fantastic picture of a ridiculously grotesque devil that stood with Gloucester on the edge:

> As I stood here below, methought his eyes
> Were two full moons; he had a thousand noses,
> Horns whelk'd and waved like the enridged sea;
> It was some fiend...   (IV. vi. 70)

Some fiend, indeed.

There is masterful artistry in all this. The Gloucester-theme has throughout run separate from that of Lear, yet parallel, and continually giving us direct villainy where the other shows cold callousness; horrors of physical torment where the other has a subtle mental torment; culminating in this towering stroke of the grotesque and absurd to balance the fantastic incidents and speeches that immediately follow. At this point we suddenly have our first sight of Lear in the full ecstasy of his later madness. Now, when our imaginations are most powerfully quickened to the grotesque and incongruous, the whole surge of the Gloucester-theme, which has just reached its climax, floods as a tributary the main stream of our sympathy with Lear. Our vision has thus been uniquely focused to understand that vision of the grotesque, the incongruous, the fantastically-horrible, which is the agony of Lear's mind:

> *(Enter* Lear, *fantastically dressed with wild flowers.)*
>
> (IV. vi. 81)

So runs Capell's direction. Lear, late "every inch a king," the supreme pathetic figure of literature, now utters the wild and whirling language of furthest madness. Sometimes his words hold profound meaning. Often they are tuned to the orthodox Shakespearian hate and loathing, especially sex-loathing, of the hate-theme. Or again, they are purely ludicrous, or would be, were it not a Lear who speaks them:

> …Look, look, a mouse! Peace, peace; this piece of toasted cheese will do't…
>
> (IV. vi. 90)

It is certainly as well that we have been by now prepared for the grotesque. Laughter is forbidden us. Consummate art has so forged plot and incident that we may watch with tears rather than laughter the cruelly comic actions of Lear:

> *Lear.* I will die bravely, like a bridegroom.[2] What!
>   I will be jovial: come, come; I am a king,
>   My masters, know you that?
> *Gentleman.* You are a royal one, and we obey you.
> *Lear.* Then there's life in't. Nay, if you get it, you shall get it with
>   running. Sa, sa, sa, sa.   (IV. vi. 203)

Lear is a child again in his madness. We are in touch with the exquisitely pathetic, safeguarded only by Shakespeare's masterful technique from the bathos of comedy.

This recurring and vivid stress on the incongruous and the fantastic is not a subsidiary element in *King Lear:* it is the very heart of the play. We watch humanity grotesquely tormented, cruelly and with mockery impaled: nearly all the persons suffer some form of crude indignity in the course of the play. I have noticed the major

---

[2]This is to be related to *Antony and Cleopatra,* IV. xii. 100, and *Measure for Measure,* III. i. 82; also *Hamlet,* IV. iv. 62.

themes of Lear and Gloucester: there are others. Kent is banished, undergoes the disguise of a servant, is put to shame in the stocks; Cornwall is killed by his own servant resisting the dastardly mutilation of Gloucester; Oswald, the prim courtier, is done to death by Edgar in the role of an illiterate country yokel—

> …keep out, che vor ye, or ise try whether your costard or my ballow
> be the harder…   (IV. vi. 247)

Edgar himself endures the utmost degradation of his disguise as "poor Tom," begrimed and naked, and condemned to speak nothing but idiocy. Edmund alone steers something of an unswerving tragic course, brought to a fitting, deserved, but spectacular end, slain by his wronged brother, nobly repentant at the last:

> *Edmund.* What you have charged me with, that have I done;
>   And more, much more; the time will bring it out:
>   'Tis past, and so am I. But what art thou
>   That hast this fortune on me? If thou'rt noble,
>   I do forgive thee.
> *Edgar.*   Let's exchange charity.
>   I am no less in blood than thou art, Edmund;
>   If more, the more thou hast wrong'd me.
>   My name is Edgar…   (V. iii. 164)

The note of forgiving chivalry reminds us of the deaths of Hamlet and Laertes. Edmund's fate is nobly tragic: "the wheel has come full circle; I am here" (V. iii. 176). And Edmund is the most villainous of all. Again, we have incongruity; and again, the Gloucester-theme reflects the Lear-theme. Edmund is given a noble, an essentially tragic, end, and Goneril and Regan, too, meet their ends with something of tragic fineness in pursuit of their evil desires. Regan dies by her sister's poison; Goneril with a knife. They die, at least, in the cause of love—love of Edmund. Compared with these deaths, the end of Cordelia is horrible, cruel, unnecessarily cruel—the final grotesque horror in the play. Her villainous sisters are already dead. Edmund is nearly dead, repentant. It is a matter of seconds—and rescue comes too late. She is hanged by a common soldier. The death which Dostoievsky's Stavrogin singled out as of all the least heroic and picturesque, or rather, shall we say, the most hideous and degrading: this is the fate that grips the white innocence and resplendent love-strength of Cordelia. To be hanged, after the death of her enemies, in the midst of friends. It is the last hideous joke of destiny: this—and the fact that Lear is still alive, has recovered his sanity for this. The death of Cordelia is the last and most horrible of all the horrible incongruities I have noticed:

> Why should a dog, a horse, a rat have life,
> And thou no breath at all?
>
> (V. iii. 308)

We remember: "Upon such sacrifices, my Cordelia, the gods themselves throw incense" (V. iii. 20). Or do they laugh, and is the *Lear* universe one ghastly piece of fun?

We do not feel that. The tragedy is most poignant in that it is purposeless, unreasonable. It is the most fearless artistic facing of the ultimate cruelty of things in our literature. That cruelty would be less were there not this element of comedy which I have emphasized, the insistent incongruities, which create and accompany the madness of Lear, which leap to vivid shape in the mockery of Gloucester's suicide, which are intrinsic in the texture of the whole play. Mankind is, as it were, deliberately and comically tormented by "the gods." He is not even allowed to die tragically. Lear is "bound upon a wheel of fire" and only death will end the victim's agony:

> Vex not his ghost: O, let him pass! he hates him
> That would upon the rack of this tough world
> Stretch him out longer.
>
> (V. iii. 315)

King Lear is supreme in that, in this main theme, it faces the very absence of tragic purpose: wherein it is profoundly different from *Timon of Athens.* Yet, as we close the sheets of this play, there is no horror, no resentment. The tragic purification of the essentially untragic is yet complete.

Now in this essay it will, perhaps, appear that I have unduly emphasized one single element of the play, magnifying it, and leaving the whole distorted. It has been my purpose to emphasize. I have not exaggerated. The pathos has not been minimized: it is redoubled. Nor does the use of the words "comic" and "humour" here imply disrespect to the poet's purpose: rather I have used these words, crudely no doubt, to cut out for analysis the very heart of the play—the thing that man dares scarcely face: the demonic grin of the incongruous and absurd in the most pitiful of human struggles with an iron fate. It is this that wrenches, splits, gashes the mind till it utters the whirling vapourings of lunacy. And, though love and music—twin sisters of salvation—temporarily may heal the racked consciousness of Lear, yet, so deeply planted in the facts of our life is this unknowing ridicule of destiny, that the uttermost tragedy of the incongruous ensues, and there is no hope save in the broken heart and limp body of death. This is of all the most agonizing of tragedies to endure: and if we are to feel more than a fraction of this agony, we must have sense of this quality of grimmest humour. We must beware of sentimentalizing the cosmic mockery of the play.

And is there, perhaps, even a deeper, and less heart-searing, significance in its humour? Smiles and tears are indeed most curiously interwoven here. Gloucester was saved from his violent and tragic suicide that he might recover his wronged son's love, and that his heart might

> 'Twixt two extremes of passion, joy and grief,
> Burst smilingly.   (V. iii. 200)

Lear dies with the words

> Do you see this? Look on her, look, her lips,
> Look there, look there!   (V. iii. 312)

What smiling destiny is this he sees at the last instant of racked mortality? Why have we that strangely beautiful account of Cordelia's first hearing of her father's pain:

> ...patience and sorrow strove
> Who should express her goodliest. You have seen
> Sunshine and rain at once: her smiles and tears
> Were like a better way: those happy smilets,
> That play'd on her ripe lip, seem'd not to know
> What guests were in her eyes; which parted thence,
> As pearls from diamonds dropp'd. In brief,
> Sorrow would be a rarity most beloved,
> If all could so become it.   (IV. iii. 18)

What do we touch in these passages? Sometimes we know that all human pain holds beauty, that no tear falls but it dews some flower we cannot see. Perhaps humour, too, is inwoven in the universal pain, and the enigmatic silence holds not only an unutterable sympathy, but also the ripples of an impossible laughter whose flight is not for the wing of human understanding; and perhaps it is this that casts its darting shadow of the grotesque across the furrowed pages of *King Lear*.

Edmund and the Two Natures

by John F. Danby

The idea of Nature,...in orthodox Elizabethan thought, is always something normative for human beings. It is impossible to talk about Nature without talking also about pattern and ideal form; about Reason as displayed in Nature; about Law as the innermost expression of Nature; about Custom which is the basis of Law and equally with Law an expression of Nature's pattern; about Restraint as the observance of Law, and the way to discover our richest self-fulfilment. In the sixteenth century the forces which have produced our view of Nature were, of course, already at work. *King Lear* finds room in its world for the Nature which is no kindly Dame but the shattering power of Thunder. But the orthodox and benignant view is also strongly represented. It is the view of those in the play who seem already to be slightly old-fashioned, but who are nevertheless unquestionably the most human.

A change in the meaning of Reason accompanies the change in the meaning of Nature. The dualism of Reason *versus* the Passions is useless to explain Edmund. Though Edmund is Appetite, he is also a rationalist. It is only that Reason for him is something different from the Reason of Lear or Gloster. Reason, of course, is another concept the orthodox never separated from God and Nature. In the contrasted views of Edmund and Gloster concerning our relations to "the Stars" the two Reasons voice themselves [I. ii. 112-44 — ed.] ....

Gloster's "wisdom of Nature" I take to mean "the scientific ac-

This selection is composed of excerpts from "The Two Natures" by John F. Danby. From *Shakespeare's Doctrine of Nature: A Study of King Lear* (London: Faber and Faber Ltd., 1948), pp. 21, 36-42, 44-46, 48-50. Copyright 1948 by Faber and Faber Ltd. Reprinted by permission of the publisher.

count of natural happenings": the sort of explanation Cicero gives in *Julius Caesar* of the miracle-charged thunder-storm over Rome the night Caesar is murdered. Gloster clings for his own part, however, to a view which sees physical nature as more than a realm of indifferent law. The eclipses are not efficient causes in a closed natural sphere of efficient causes: that is how Edmund regards them. They are not even efficient causes of the catastrophes that seem to accompany them. They are symptoms of a disease which affects all nature. And the disease is bound to break out in man's world too.

Edmund, on the other hand, admits of no connections in Nature save connections of material cause and effect. And Nature is a closed system. For him, as for us, it is a structure laid down, devoid of intelligence, impervious to Reason. This being so it is ridiculous to blame the stars for one's misfortunes. Nature is dead mechanism, and it does not include man, except as he is an animal body. Apart from his body, man has a mind. As mind, man is free of nature and superior to it. He knows its laws, he can manipulate it for a given effect. Human nature, too, can be known and manipulated. The machiavel will know it better than anyone else, and he will be freer to manipulate it. It is significant that in the figure of Edmund the sense of separation from nature and superiority to it goes with a sense of the individual's separation from the community and a feeling of superiority to his fellows. As Nature goes dead, community becomes competition, and man a nexus of appetites. Reason is no longer a normative drive but a calculator of the means to satisfy the appetites with which we were born.

Edmund's philosopher, we have said, is Hobbes—born in the Armada year and surviving to philosophise into the Restoration. Hobbes's vision of man in society is the projection on to a philosophic plane of Edmund, Goneril, and Regan....

> *Goneril.* This man hath had good counsel, a hundred knights?
>   'Tis politic, and safe to let him keep
>   At point a hundred knights: yes, that on every dream,
>   Each buzz, each fancy, each complaint, dislike,
>   He may enguard his dotage with their powers,
>   And hold our lives in mercy....
> *Albany.* Well, you may fear too far.
> *Goneril.* Safer than trust too far;
>   Let me still take away the harms I fear,
>   Not fear still to be taken.   (I. iv.)

It might be noted in passing that here again (it is obvious in
Edmund's first soliloquy) characters are shown taking decisions.
And the field of choice is tense with important alternatives. *King
Lear* makes more use of deliberate choice as a means of characterization than any other of Shakespeare's plays with the possible exception of *Antony and Cleopatra.* The effect of this on characterization
is immediate. None of the characters are complex, yet each has an
unmistakeable richness of significance and an emphatic vitality.
The richness and vitality come from the way in which they are related, through decision, to the abruptly contoured Nature which
forms the general background. The richness is a matter of the profound or horrifying overtones which the context of Nature provides.
The characters thus call for the same kind of treatment as the characters of Morality. They are not Morality-figures. They stand one
stage nearer to actuality than the personages of allegory. The clear
Morality outline is however included in the play. The unambiguous
Morality statement is presented in the deliberate stance each character adopts in the clearly-marked field. Thus Albany in this passage is obviously the voice of Nature in the benevolent sense of
Hooker. Goneril is expressing Hobbes's alternative. What each says
is "common sense." It is only through their vivid juxtaposition here
that we are made to realize how far common sense itself is merely
the afterbirth of decisions, acts of choice already made. Common
sense will take one down the dip-slope, the other down the scarp-
slope from this divide. Two persons are contrasted, but also two
natures, two destinies for man. Throughout the play we are constantly prevented from taking a local view of the situation developing. The play presents the fate of man, the situation of man, in
general.

The key-word in Goneril's speech is "politic." By it Shakespeare
reminds his audience of the race of machiavels he has been deal-
ing with since *Henry VI.* He points also to a constant challenge to
a whole range of meanings which his generation felt to be a serious
one. Goneril's other word is "dotage." By this her common sense
forces us to examine the presuppositions of any common sense we
would, with Albany, oppose to hers. By it she forces us out of the
comfortable static positions of common sense. We are made to review the acts of choice our common sense depends on—and their
implications.

The "three principal causes of quarrel" in human nature Hobbes
found to be "competition, diffidence, glory": the impulse to acquire,

to provide for one's security, to extend one's prestige. Edmund and the two sisters are made to a recipe equally simple. All that needs to be added to Hobbes in order to account for them is lust. We have described their characters as soon as we have itemized these ingredients. One detail in the picture of the sisters, however, might be pointed to. Bradley does not overlook it, but does not, I think, sufficiently stress it. It is an indication of Shakespeare's conscious concern with the abstract theme in the play. The information has little dramatic relevance at the point where it occurs. Its whole force comes from the way in which it links up with the play's intellectual content.—Before Edmund meets them, and before the rejection of Lear has been contemplated, war between the sisters is already rumoured as imminent. It is as if Shakespeare were underlining the Hobbesian account of human nature, its inherent competitiveness based on fear, its mechanical "every man against every man." The Hobbesian conception needs for its embodiment at least *two* daughters. As characters these will have to be practically indistinguishable: they will be at odds because of their alikeness. Allegory need go no further....

Edmund in his opening soliloquy is the compact image of everything that denies the orthodox view. Shakespeare thought of him simply and inclusively as the Bastard, and "bastard" is the Elizabethan equivalent of "outsider." Edmund is a complete Outsider. He is outside Society, he is outside Nature, he is outside Reason. Man, Nature, and God now fall apart. Reason, for Hooker the principle of coherence for all three, dwindles to something regulative rather than constitutive. It is an analyser, a cold calculator. Its knowledge is the knowledge of the watchmaker or engineer, an understanding of cogs and springs and levers, of mining and counter-mining. Nature itself becomes a machine this Reason can have this knowledge of. Descartes' dualism is implicit in Edmund's reasoning on the stars. The New Man is a Mind and a Body. The body belongs to mechanical Lion-headed Nature. The mind stands outside as observer and server of the machine.

In Edmund, ... politic machiavel and renaissance scientist—two vast images—are fused. In addition Edmund is the careerist on the make, the New Man laying a mine under the crumbling walls and patterned streets of an ageing society that thinks it can disregard him. For the two Natures and two Reasons imply two societies. Edmund belongs to the new age of scientific inquiry and industrial development, of bureaucratic organization and social regimentation, the age of mining and merchant-venturing, of monopoly and Empire-making, the age of the sixteenth century and after: an age of competition, suspicion, glory. He hypostatizes those trends in man which guarantee success under the new conditions—one reason why his soliloquy is so full of what we recognize as common sense. These trends he calls Nature. And with this Nature he identifies Man. Edmund would not agree that any other Nature was thinkable.

Another Nature was being asserted, however, in Edmund's time, because there was another society not yet outgrown. This is the society of the sixteenth century and before. The standards Edmund rejects have come down from the Middle Ages. They assume a co-operative, reasonable decency in man, and respect for the whole as being greater than the part: "God to be worshipped, parents to be honoured, others to be used by us as we ourselves would be by them." The medieval procedure was to mutualize conflicting claims by agreeing over limits. Edmund's instinct is to recognize no limits save those coming from incapacity to get one's way....

Edmund is the New Man. Shakespeare's understanding of the type is so extensive as to amount to real sympathy. The insight comes, I think, from Shakespeare's being in part a New Man himself. This would account for the colour and charm with which he always invests the figure. Be that as it may, Shakespeare has had ample time to observe that which he embodies in Edmund. Edmund is not a theory of human nature only, though his existence demands one. He is a fact. To inquire into the meaning he gives to "Nature" is not merely to hunt for a new dictionary meaning. Nor in handling the old and the new meanings is Shakespeare writing an academic thesis. The ideas are people. The meanings are moving bits of a changing world. Behind the shift and drift of the meanings of the word "Nature" there is the shift and drift of humanity in a setting at once historical and spiritual. Behind the word there is Shakespeare certainly. But behind Shakespeare there is the mining engineer breaking into the bowels of the earth; the seeker out of the mysteries of brass, and glass, and salt, and the supplier of the Elizabethan navies; the doctor taking apart the human body to anatomize the mechanism of muscle and bone; the capitalist aware of money as the sinews of war and soon to recognize in it the circulating life-blood of the body politic. All these, too, are vitally concerned to alter the meaning of Nature: to extend the Nature which can be worked, made a tool of, got to produce profits; to minimize the theology which would contend for an aesthetic and moral attitude only to Nature, and which would find no argument in Nature for profit-making.

There is tremendous gusto in the portrait of the Bastard: energy, emancipation, a right-minded scorn of humbug, clear-headedness; the speed, sureness, and lissom courage of a tiger. Edmund is the last great expression in Shakespeare of that side of Renaissance individualism which has made a positive addition to the heritage of the West. After *King Lear* the figure does not appear again. This is because, I think, in *King Lear* Shakespeare gives a final and exhaustive statement to the issues he has been handling throughout his chronicles since *Henry VI*. But in spite of the attractiveness of the portrait, Edmund still belongs with Goneril and Regan. He is a Shakespearian villain. And condemned with him in the apocalyptical judgment of the play is the corrupt society he represents.

The World of *King Lear*

by Maynard Mack

To turn from a play's action to its world is not, when the dramatist is Shakespeare, to take up a new subject but to reconsider the old in a new light. The strains of violence and aggression stressed earlier in connection with the play's action could as well be treated as an aspect of its world. The bareness and spareness so often cited as features of its world penetrate equally the character and action. The austerity and rigor that these have in *King Lear* may best be appreciated by comparing Hal and Falstaff, in whom the dramatist's exuberant invention multiplies variety, to Lear and his Fool, where invention plays intensely but always along the same arc; or by recalling *Othello*, with all its supernumerary touches of actual domesticity in Desdemona, actual concerns of state in the Moor; or *Hamlet*, with its diversions and digressions among guardsmen, recorders, gossip of city theatres, its mass of historical and literary allusions, its diversities of witty, sophisticated, and self-conscious speech. Lear, too, contains diversities of speech—ritual and realistic styles described by W. B. C. Watkins,[1] iterations singled out by Bradley to characterize Cordelia[2] (which are, in fact, characteristic of several of the play's speakers), "oracular fragments of rhapsody" in the mad scenes (the phrase is Granville-Barker's),[3] imperatives, preachments, questionings, and, last but not least, the Fool's wry idiom,

"The World of *King Lear*" (editor's title). From Maynard Mack, "Action and World," in *King Lear in Our Time* (Berkeley and Los Angeles: University of California press, 1965), pp. 98-117. Copyright © 1965 by The Regents of the University of California. Reprinted by permission of the University of California Press.

[1]"The Two Techniques in *King Lear*," *Review of English Studies*, XVIII (1942), 1-26, reprinted in enlarged form as chap. iii of his *Shakespeare and Spenser* (1950).

[2]*Lectures on Shakespearean Tragedy* (1904), p. 319; he is corrected on this point by Granville-Barker (*Prefaces to Shakespeare*, I, 281).

[3]*Ibid.*

vehicle of the hard-won wisdom of the poor, made up largely of proverb, riddle, maxim, fable, and ballad. *Lear* has such diversities, but as Winifred Nowottny argues convincingly in a recent essay, all are marked, even the most passionate and poignant, by a surface "absence of contrivance,"[4] which allows flashes of profound feeling to flare up unexpectedly in the most unpretentious forms of speech, yet seems to tell us at the same time (this is of course the measure of its artfulness in fact) that "feeling and suffering...are beyond words." "The play is deeply concerned," she writes, "with the inadequacy of language to do justice to feeling or to afford any handhold against abysses of iniquity and suffering."[5] Here, too, it strikes me, the play is of a piece. As it uses for the most part the barest bones of language to point at experiences that lie beyond the scope of language, so it uses stripped-down constituents of personality (character that is entirely *esse*, that does not alter but develops to be always more completely the thing it was—as in Kent, for whom banishment simply means that he will "shape his old course in a country new," and who at the end of the play will be about answering his master's call once again) to point to complexities of being and of human reality that lie beyond the scope of the ordinary conventions of dramatic character.

But these are matters that come through to us more clearly in the study than onstage. There can be no question that the most powerful single dimension of the play's world for its spectators is its continual reference to an evocation, through eye and ear alike, of the nature and significance of human society. A "sense of sympathy and human relatedness," as Miss Welsford has said, is what the good in this play have or win through to.[6] In the world of *King Lear,* this is the ultimate gift, spring of man's joy and therefore of his pain. When Lear dies, as I mentioned in the beginning, with his whole being launched toward another, with even his last gasp an expression of hope that she lives, the image before us is deeply tragic; yet it is also, in the play's terms, a kind of victory. This is a matter we must come back to. What needs to be considered first is the circumstantial "sociality" of the Lear world which defines and gives body to this closing vision of human achievement and its cost.

In writing *King Lear,* Shakespeare's imagination appears to have

---

[4]"Some Aspects of the Style of *King Lear,*" *Shakespeare Survey,* XIII (1960), 51.
[5]*Ibid.,* p. 52.
[6]*The Fool: His Social and Literary History* (1935), p. 258.

been so fully oriented toward presenting human reality as a web of ties commutual that not only characterization and action, but language, theme, and even the very *mise en scène* are influenced. The play's imagined settings—divisible into several distinct landscapes as "shadowy forests" and "champains" fade off first into "low farms and poor pelting villages," then into the bare and treeless heath, then into glimpses of high-grown grain at Dover on the brink of the giddy cliff that only exists in Edgar's speech and his father's imagination—are always emphatically social. Even on that literally and emblematically lonesome heath we are never allowed to forget the nearby presence of what Mr. Eliot calls in his *Dry Salvages* "the life of significant soil." Somewhere just beyond the storm's rim and suitably framing the rain-swept beggared king, Shakespeare evokes through Tom of Bedlam's speeches a timeless community of farms and villages where the nights are measured between "curfew" and "the first cock," the beggars are "whipp'd from tithing to tithing," the green mantle of the standing pool is broken by the castaway carcasses of the "old rat and the ditch dog," and the white wheat is mildewed by "the foul Flibbertigibbet," who also gives poor rustics "the web and the pin, squinies the eye and makes the hairlip."[7] Likewise at Dover, around the two old men, one mad, one blind, Shakespeare raises another kind of society, equally well adapted to the movement of the plot, courtly, sophisticated, decadent. A society of adulterers and "simp'ring dames." A society where "a dog's obey'd in office," the beadle lusts for the whore he whips, "the usurer hangs the cozener," and "robes and furr'd gowns hides all."

It is by these surrealist backgrounds and conflations, as we all know, that Shakespeare dilates his family story into a parable of society of all times and places. The characters, too, bear some signs of having been shaped with such a parable in view. As a group, they are significantly representative, bringing before us both extremes of a social and political spectrum (monarch and beggar), a psychic spectrum (wise man and fool), a moral spectrum (beastly behavior and angelic), an emotional spectrum (joy and despair), and, through out, a "contrast of dimension," as Miss Nowottny has called it,[8] that draws within one compass both the uttermost human anguish which speaks in "She's dead as earth" and the strange limiting "art of our

---

[7]Evoked also, of course, is the society of Edgar's imagined corrupt past, a society of "brothels," "plackets," "lenders' books," etc.

[8]*Op. cit.*, p. 56.

necessities" which speaks in "Undo this button." As individuals, on
the other hand, these same characters, especially the younger ones,
show a significant and perhaps studied diversification. According to
one producer of the play, we meet with "heartless intellect" in Edmund, "impure feelings" in Goneril, "unenlightened will" in Cornwall, "powerless morality" in Albany, "unimaginative mediocrity"
in Regan.[9] I should not care myself to adopt these particular descriptions, but they serve to call attention to what everyone has
recognized to be a somewhat schematic variety in the play's *dramatis
personae,* as if the playwright were concerned to exhibit the widest
possible range of human potentiality. This general "anatomy" of
mankind, if it is such, is further enhanced by the well-known anti-
phonal characterizations of Lear and Gloucester and even by the
double quality of the old king himself as Titan and (in Cordelia's
phrase) "poor *perdu.*" Thus, from the play's opening moments,
when we are shown all the powers of the realm collected and glimpse
both aspects of the king, we are never allowed to lose sight of the fact
that the people in front of us make up a composite image of the state
of man, in every sense of the word "state."

Shakespeare's concern with "relation" as the ultimate reality for
human beings also expresses itself strongly in the plot of *King Lear*
and in the language of social use and habit to which the plot gives
rise and which it repeatedly examines. To an extent unparalleled
in the other tragedies, the plot of the play depends on and manipulates relations of service and of family—the two relations, as W. H.
Auden has reminded us in an arresting essay, from which all human
loyalties, and therefore all societies, derive.[10] Family ties, which
come about by nature, cannot be dissolved by acts of will: in this lies
the enormity of Lear's action in the opening scene and of his elder
daughters' actions later. Service ties, however, being contractual,
can be dissolved by acts of will, only the act must be ratified on both
sides. Kent, refusing to dissolve his relation with his master, illustrates the crucial difference between the two types of affiliation.
The essentials of the service bond can be restored even though Kent
is unrecognized and in disguise. The essentials of the natural bond
between Cordelia and Lear, or Edgar and Gloucester, can never be
restored apart from mutual recognition and a change of heart.

[9] Michael Chekhov, *To the Actor on the Technique of Acting* (1953), p. 134.

[10] "Balaam and His Ass," *The Dyer's Hand* (1962), pp. 107-108.

Ties of service and ties of nature lie closely parallel in *King Lear* and sometimes merge. It has been argued that one way of interpreting the broad outlines of the story would be to say that the lesson King Lear must learn includes the lesson of true service, which is necessarily part of the lesson of true love.[11] Once Lear has banished true love and true service in the persons of Cordelia and Kent, it is only to be expected that he will have trouble with false service and false love in a variety of forms, including Oswald, his daughters, and his knights, and that he should need, once again, the intercession of true service in the form of the disguised Kent. Gloucester, too, we are told, has to learn to distinguish true service. Beginning by serving badly, he is badly served in turn by Edmund, and only after he becomes a true servant, going to Lear's rescue at the risk of his life, is he himself once more served truly, first by his old tenant, and subsequently by Edgar.

The term "service," with its cognates and synonyms, tolls in the language of *King Lear* like that bell which reminded John Donne we are all parts of a single continent, but it is only one of a host of socially oriented terms to do so. Almost as prominent, and equally pertinent to the playwright's concern with human relatedness, are the generic terms of social responsibility: "meet," "fit," "proper," "due," "duty," "bond," and the generic appellations of social status and social approbation and disapprobation: "knave," "fool," "villain," "rogue," "rascal," "slave," and many more. Often these last are simply vehicles of the willfulness that crackles in this frantic disintegrating realm where kings are beggars, but several of them carry in solution anxious questions about the ties that hold together the human polity, which from time to time the action of the play precipitates out. When Cornwall, challenged by his own servant after Gloucester's blinding, exclaims incredulously "My villain!" and Regan adds scornfully "A peasant stand up thus!" the ambiguities that may attach to servitude are brought into question with a precision that enables us to appreciate the immediately following references to Gloucester as "treacherous villain" and "eyeless villain," and to the now slain rebel servant as "this slave." In the Byam Shaw production, as Muriel St. Clare Byrne describes it, a highly imaginative *exeunt* was adopted for Regan and Cornwall at this moment, which must have brought home to any audience the im-

---

[11] Jonas Barish and Marshall Waingrow, "'Service' in *King Lear*," *Shakespeare Quarterly*, IX (1958), 347-355.

plications of a world in which language could be so perversely and solipsistically misused. "Mortally wounded, terror and pain in voice and gesture, Cornwall turned to his wife: 'Regan, I bleed apace. Give me your arm.' Ignoring him, almost disdainfully, she swept past to the downstage exit. He staggered back, groping for support; no one stirred to help him. Open-mouthed, staring-eyed, death griping his heart, he faced the dawning horror of retribution as the jungle law of each for himself caught up on him and he knew himself abandoned even by his wife."[12]

Two other "titles" that the play first manipulates and then explores in visually expressive episodes are "gentleman" and "fellow." Kent is introduced to us and to Edmund as "this noble gentleman" in the first lines of the play, a title which he later amplifies into "gentleman of blood and breeding." Oswald is also introduced to us first as a gentleman — "my gentleman" — by Goneril, and receives the title again at a significant moment when Edgar, speaking as a peasant, has to defend his father's life against him. In II, ii, these two very different definitions of gentility, Oswald and Kent, clash outside Gloucester's castle. The "gentleman of blood and breeding" puts Goneril's "gentleman" to rout by power of nature, but by power of authority — that great graven image of authority which, as Lear says later in a reference likely to recall this episode, makes "the creature run from the cur" — he is ejected (and punished) in favor of one whose true titles, Kent tells us, make him no gentleman, but "the composition of a knave, beggar, coward, pandar, and the son and heir of a mongrel bitch."

Or again, the play asks (and this is perhaps its most searching exploration visually as well as verbally), what is it that makes a man a "fellow"? Is it being born to menial status, as for the many serving-men to whom the word is applied? Is it total loss of status, as for Edgar, Kent, and Lear, to each of whom the word is also applied? Or is it simply being man — everyone's fellow by virtue of a shared humanity? During the heath scenes, when Lear, Kent, Edgar, and the Fool become fellows in misery as well as in lack of status, this question too is given a poignant visual statement. Gloucester, coming to relieve Lear, rejects one member of the motley fellowship, his own son Poor Tom: "In, fellow, there into the hovel." But Lear, who has just learned to pray for all such naked fellows, refuses to be separated from his new companion and finally is allowed to "take

[12]*King Lear* at Stratford-on-Avon, 1959," *Shakespeare Quarterly*, XI (1960), 198.

the fellow" into shelter with him. For, as Edgar will ask us to remember in the next scene but one,

> the mind much sufferance doth o'erskip,
> When grief hath mates, and bearing fellowship.

Questions like these point ultimately to larger and more abstract
questions, over which the action of the play, like Hamlet's melan-
choly, "sits on brood." One of these has to do with the moral founda-
tions of society. To what extent have our distinctions of degree and
status, our regulations by law and usage, moral significance? To
what extent are they simply the expedient disguises of a war of all
on all, wherein humanity preys on itself (as Albany says) "Like
monsters of the deep"? This anxiety, though it permeates the play,
is pressed with particular force in the utterances of the mad king to
Gloucester in the fields near Dover. Here, as so often in Shakespeare, we encounter an occasion when the barriers between fiction
and reality are suddenly collapsed, and the Elizabethan audience
was made to realize, as we are, that it was listening to an indictment
far more relevant to its own social experience than to any this king
of ancient Britain could be imagined to have had. Furthermore,
here onstage, as during the scene on the heath, a familiar conven-
tion was again being turned upside down and made electric with
meaning. A king of the realm—like their own king, guarantee of its
coinage ("they cannot touch me for coining"), commander of its
troops ("There's your press money"), chief object of its *paideia*
("They flattered me like a dog"), fountain of its justice ("I pardon
that man's life"), center of its reverence ("O! let me kiss that hand")—
was not only presented mad, crowned with weeds, but in his madness registered for all to hear the bankruptcy of the very body
politic (and body moral) of which he was representative and head:

> Plate sin with gold,
> And the strong lance of justice hurtless breaks;
> Arm it in rags, a pigmy's straw does pierce it.
> None does offend, none, I say none; I'll able 'em:
> Take that of me, my friend, who have the power
> To seal th' accuser's lips. Get thee glass eyes;
> And, like a scurvy politician, seem
> To see the things thou dost not.

No one, I suspect, who had responded to the role of the king in
Shakespeare's history plays, or the king's role in contemporary

drama generally, could miss the shock in these lines, coming as they did from "the thing itself." If we suppose, further, that the structural conventions of the Elizabethan theatre, with its "very solid three-dimensional symbols of order" representing "home, city, and king,"[13] sometimes induced in observers a deeper identification, a sense that they were witnessing in the career of the stage monarch a "sacred combat" or ritual struggle that enacted the corporate (and individual) quest for well-being and self-knowledge in the person of the king, we may guess that the shock of this reversal was profound indeed. But we need not suppose so much. Even the most casual playgoer, who had looked about him reflectively in Jacobean England, must have experienced a shudder of self-recognition as Lear's "sermon" proceeded. The gulf between medieval social ideals and contemporary actualities was imposing by Shakespeare's time a significant strain on sensitive minds, the kind of strain that (in a way we are painfully familiar with in our own age) can madden men, as in a sense it has maddened Lear. "The ideal was still Christian," writes Crane Brinton, who has put the matter as pithily as anyone, "still an ideal of unity, peace, security, organization, status; the reality was endemic war, divided authority even at the top, [and] a great scramble for wealth and position."[14]

Lear's vision of society in Dover fields is a vision of this gulf. To a limited extent it relates to his own sufferings, but principally to the society for which it was written, and, I would wish to add, to all societies as such. Under the masks of disipline, Lear's speeches imply, in any imaginable society on earth, there will always lurk the lust of the simpering dame, the insolence of the dog in office, the hypocrisy of the usurer who hangs the cozener, the mad injustice of sane men's choices, like Lear's in disowning Cordelia. Institutions are necessary if society is to exist at all; but as the play here eloquently points out, and as Lear from this point on himself knows, they are not enough.[15] What human relatedness truly means, stripped of its robes and furr'd gowns and all marks of status and images of authority, we are shown in the ensuing scenes of mutual humility and compassion between Lear and Cordelia, Edgar and Gloucester.

[13]G. R. Kernodle, "The Open Stage: Elizabethan or Existentialist," *Shakespeare Survey*, XII (1959), 3.

[14]*Ideas and Men* (1950), p. 269.

[15]See particularly on this point Arthur Sewell, *Character and Society in Shakespeare* (1951), pp. 110 ff.

A second question that the play keeps bringing before our imaginations in its social dimension is the problem of human identity. It sees this, in part, as a function of status, and it is doubtless not without meaning that so many of the play's persons undergo drastic alterations in the "statistical" sphere. Cordelia is deprived of her place in state and family; Kent, of his earldom; Edgar, of his sonship and patrimony; Gloucester, of his title and lands; Lear, of the whole fabric of familiar relations by which he has always known himself to be Lear and through the loss of which he falls into madness. Yet the matter is also presented to us at a deeper level than that of status. When, at Goneril's Lear cries out, "This is not Lear. ... Who is it that can tell me who I am?" or, on the heath, staring at Edgar's nakedness, "Is man no more than this?" we realize that his questionings cast a shadow well beyond the limits of the immediate situation as he understands it, a shadow that involves the problem of human identity in its ultimate sense, which has lost none of its agonizing ambiguity with the passage of three centuries. *Is* man, in fact, no more than "this"? — a poor bare forked animal in the wind and rain — or is man a metaphysical conception, a normative term, which suffers violence whenever any human being has been reduced to the condition of "bare fork'd animal," whenever "man's life is cheap as beast's" because the "need" has been too much "reasoned," whenever "man's work" (as with Edmund's officer) excludes drawing a cart or eating dried oats but not the murder of his own kind? As the waters rise against our foothold on the cliff of chalk, this has become our question too.

The ultimate uncertainty in *King Lear* to which all others point is, as always in tragedy, the question of man's fate. With its strong emphasis on inexorable and unimaginable consequences unwinding to make a web to which every free and willful act contributes another toil, *King Lear* may claim a place near the absolute center, "the true blank" (so Kent might call it) of tragic experience. "The tragedy of Adam," writes Northrop Frye, following Milton in tracing "the archetypal human tragedy" in the narrative of Genesis, "resolves, like all other tragedies, in the manifestation of natural law. He enters a world in which existence is itself tragic, not existence modified by an act, deliberate or unconscious."[16] This is the form of tragedy I think we all sense at the basis of *King Lear*, and the reason

[16]*Anatomy of Criticism* (1957), pp. 212, 213.

why its windows opening on the pilgrimage and *psychomachia* of a king who is also Rex Humanitas are so relevant to its theme. Existence is tragic in *King Lear* because existence is inseparable from relation; we are born from and to it; it envelops us in our loves and lives as parents, children, sisters, brothers, husbands, wives, servants, masters, rulers, subjects—the web is seamless and unending. When we talk of virtue, patience, courage, joy, we talk of what supports it. When we talk of tyranny, lust, and treason, we talk of what destroys it. There is no human action, Shakespeare shows us, that does not affect it and that it does not affect. Old, we begin our play with the need to impose relation—to divide our kingdom, set our rest on someone's kind nursery, and crawl toward our death. Young, we begin it with the need to respond to relation—to define it, resist it even in order to protect it, honor it, or destroy it. Man's tragic fate, as *King Lear* presents it, comes into being with his entry into relatedness, which is his entry into humanity.

In the play's own terms this fate is perhaps best summarized in the crucial concept of "patience." By the time he meets Gloucester in Dover fields, Lear has begun to learn patience; and patience, as he defines it now, is not at all what he had earlier supposed. He had supposed it was the capacity to bear up under the outrages that occur in a corrupt world to oneself; and so he had cried, when Regan and Goneril joined forces against him, "You heavens, give me that patience, patience I need!" Now, with his experience of the storm behind him, his mind still burning with the lurid vision of a world where "None does offend, none," because all are guilty, he sees further. His subject is not personal suffering in what he here says to Gloucester; his subject is the suffering that is rooted in the very fact of being human, and its best symbol is the birth cry of every infant, as if it knew already that to enter humanity is to be born in pain, to suffer pain, and to cause pain.

> Thou must be patient; we came crying hither:
> Thou know'st the first time that we smell the air
> We waul and cry.

Or as George Gascoigne had put it, giving an old sentiment a new turn in his translation of Innocent III's *De Contemptu Mundi*: "We are all borne crying that we may thereby expresse our misery; for a male childe lately borne pronounceth A [for Adam] and a woman childe pronounceth E [for Eve] : So that they say eyther E or A: as many as discend from Eva. . . . Eche of these soundes is the voyce of a sorrowful creature, expressing the greatnesse of his grefe."[17]

Lear's words to Gloucester, I take it, describe this ultimate dimension of patience, in which the play invites us to share at its close. It is the patience to accept the condition of being human in a scheme of things where the thunder will not peace at our bidding; where nothing can stay the unfolding consequences of a rash act, including the rash acts of bearing and being born;

> where the worst is not
> So long as we can say 'This is the worst';

yet where the capacity to grow and ripen — in relation and in love — is in some mysterious way bound up with the capacity to lose, and to suffer, and to endure:

> Men must endure
> Their going hence, even as their coming hither:
> Ripeness is all.

From one half of this tragic knowledge, Lear subsequently wavers — as Gloucester wavers from what Edgar thought he had learned at Dover Cliff. Lear would need no crumbs of comfort after the battle if his sufferings could at last be counted on to bring rewards — if, for example, he could pass his declining years in peace and happiness with Cordelia. He wants to believe that this is possible. He has made the choice that he should have made in the beginning. He has allied himself with those who in the world's sense are fools; and he is prepared to accept the alienation from the world that this requires, as the famous passage at the opening of the last scene shows. In this passage he puts aside Goneril and Regan forever; he does not even want to see them. He accepts eagerly the prison which marks his withdrawal from the world's values, for he has his own new values to sustain:

> We two alone will sing like birds i' th' cage:
> When thou dost ask me blessing, I'll kneel down
> And ask of thee forgiveness: so we'll live,
> And pray, and sing, and tell old tales, and laugh
> At gilded butterflies, and hear poor rogues
> Talk of court news; and we'll talk with them too,
> Who loses and who wins, who's in, who's out:
> And take upon 's the mystery of things
> As if we were God's spies.

[17]*Complete Works*, ed. J. W. Cunliffe (1910), II, 220.

They will be in the world, but not of it. On this kind of sacrifice, he adds, "the Gods themselves throw incense."

But to speak so is to speak from a knowledge that no human experience teaches. If it could end like this, if there were guaranteed rewards like this for making our difficult choices, the play would be a melodrama, and our world very different from what it is. So far as human wisdom goes, the choice of relatedness must be recognized as its own reward, leading sometimes to alleviation of suffering, as in the case of Gloucester's joy in Edgar, but equally often to more suffering, as in the case of Lear. For Lear, like many another, has to make the difficult choice only to lose the fruits of it. Not in his own death—as Kent says, "he hates him That would upon the rack of this tough world Stretch him out longer"—but in Cordelia's. Cordelia, our highest choice, is what we always want the gods to guarantee. But to this the gods will not consent. Hence when Albany exclaims, at Edmund's confession that he has ordered Cordelia's death, "The gods defend her," the gods' answer to that is, as Bradley pointed out long ago, "Enter Lear, with Cordelia in his arms."[18]

In his last speech, the full implications of the human condition evidently come home to Lear. He has made his choice, and there will be no reward. Again and again, in his repetitions, he seems to be trying to drive this final tragic fact into his human consciousness, where it never wants to stick:

> No, no, no life!
> Why should a dog, a horse, a rat have life
> And thou no breath at all? Thou'lt come no more,
> Never, never, never, never, never!

He tries to hold this painful vision unflinchingly before his consciousness, but the strain, considering everything else he has been through, is too great: consciousness itself starts to give way: "Pray you, undo this button: thank you, Sir." And with it the vision gives way too: he cannot sustain it; he dies, reviving in his heart the hope that Cordelia lives: "Look on her, look, her lips, Look there, look there!"

We are offered two ways of being sentimental about this conclusion, both of which we must make an effort to eschew. One is to follow those who argue that, because these last lines probably mean that

[18]*Op. cit.*, p. 326.

Lear dies in the joy of thinking Cordelia lives, some sort of mitiga-
tion or transfiguration has been reached which turns defeat into
total victory. "Only to earthbound intelligence," says Professor
O. J. Campbell, "is Lear pathetically deceived in thinking Cordelia
alive. Those familiar with the Morality plays will realize that Lear
has found in her unselfish love the one companion who is willing to
go with him through Death up to the throne of the Everlast-
ing Judge."[19] I think most of us will agree that this is too simple.
Though there is much of the Morality play in *Lear*, it is not used
toward a morality theme, but, as I have tried to suggest in this essay,
toward building a deeply metaphysical metaphor, or myth, about
the human condition, the state of man, in which the last of many
mysteries is the engimatic system of relatedness in which he
is enclosed.

The other sentimentality leads us to indulge the currently fashion-
able existentialist *nausée*, and to derive from the fact that Lear's
joy is mistaken, or, alternatively, from the fact that in the Lear world
"even those who have fully repented, done penance, and risen to
the tender regard of sainthood can be hunted down, driven insane,
and killed by the most agonizing extremes of passion,"[20] the conclusion that "we inhabit an imbecile universe."[21] Perhaps we do—
but Shakespeare's *King Lear* provides no evidence of it that till
now we lacked. That love, compassion, hope, and truth are "subjects
all," not only to "envious and calumniating time," but to purest
casualty and mischance has been the lament of poets since Homer.
Shakespeare can hardly have imagined that in *King Lear*'s last scene
he was telling his audiences something they had never known, or
was casting his solemn vote on one side or other of the vexing philosophical and theological questions involved in the suffering of the
innocent and good. The scene has, besides, his characteristic ambiguity and balance. No world beyond this one in which "all manner
of things will be well" is asserted; but neither is it denied: Kent
happens to take it for granted and will follow his master beyond
that horizon as he has beyond every other: "My master calls me,
I must not say no." Edgar has come to soberer assessments of reality
than he was given to making in the forepart of the play, but his instinctive kindness (we may assume) is unabated and has survived
all trials. Lear's joy in thinking that his daughter lives (if this is

[19]"The Salvation of Lear," *ELH*, XV (1948), 107.

[20]J. Stampfer, "The Catharsis of *King Lear*," *Shakespeare Survey*, XIII (1960), 4.

[21]*Ibid.*, p. 10.

what his words imply) is illusory, but it is one we need not begrudge
him on his deathbed, as we do not begrudge it to a dying man in
hospital whose family has just been wiped out. Nor need we draw
elaborate inferences from its illusoriness about the imbecility of
our world; in a similar instance among our acquaintances, we would
regard the illusion as a godsend, or even, if we were believers, as
God-sent.

In short, to say, with an increasing number of recent critics, that
"the remorseless process of *King Lear*" forces us to "face the fact
of its ending without any support from systems of moral...belief
at all"[22] is to indulge the mid-twentieth-century *frisson du néant*
at its most sentimental. We face the ending of this play, as we face our
world, with whatever support we customarily derive from systems
of belief or unbelief. If the sound of David crying "Absalom, my
son," the image of Mary bending over another broken child, the
motionless form of a missionary doctor whose martyrdom is recent,
not to mention all that earth has known of disease, famine, earthquake,
war, and prison since men first came crying hither—if our moral
and religious systems can survive this, and the record suggests that
for many good men they do and can, then clearly they will have no
trouble in surviving the figure of Lear as he bends in his agony,
or in his joy, above Cordelia. Tragedy never tells us what to think;
it shows us what we are and may be. And what we are and may be
was never, I submit, more memorably fixed upon a stage than in this
kneeling old man whose heartbreak is precisely the measure of what,
in our world of relatedness, it is possible to lose and possible to win.
The victory and the defeat are simultaneous and inseparable.

If there is any "remorseless process" in *King Lear*, it is one that
begs us to seek the meaning of our human fate not in what becomes
of us, but in what we become. Death, as we saw, is miscellaneous and
commonplace; it is life whose quality may be made noble and dis-
tinctive. Suffering we all recoil from; but we know it is a greater
thing to suffer than to lack the feelings and virtues that make it
possible to suffer. Cordelia, we may choose to say, accomplished
nothing, yet we know it is better to have been Cordelia than to have
been her sisters. When we come crying hither, we bring with us
the badge of all our misery; but it is also the badge of the vulnerabilities that give us access to whatever grandeur we achieve.

[22]Nicholas Brooke, *Shakespeare: King Lear* (1963), p. 60.

The Avoidance of Love

by Stanley Cavell

In a fine paper published a few years ago, Professor Paul Alpers notes the tendency of modern critics to treat metaphors or symbols rather than the characters and actions of Shakespeare's plays as primary data in understanding them, and undertakes to disconfirm a leading interpretation of the symbolic sort which exactly depends upon a neglect, even a denial, of the humanness of the play's characters.[1] If I begin by finding fault with his reading, I put him first to acknowledge my indebtedness to his work. His animus is polemical and in the end this animus betrays him. For he fails to account for the truth to which that leading interpretation is responding, and in his concern to insist that the characters of the play are human beings confronting one another, he fails to characterize them as specific persons. He begins by assembling quotations from several commentators which together comprise the view he wishes to correct—the view of the "sight pattern":

> In *King Lear* an unusual amount of imagery drawn from vision and the eyes prompts us to apprehend a symbolism of sight and blindness having its culmination in Gloucester's tragedy....The blinding of Gloucester might well be gratuitous melodrama but for its being imbedded in a field of meanings centered in the concept of *seeing*. This sight pattern relentlessly brings into the play the problem of seeing and what is always implied is that the problem is one of insight....It is commonly recognized that just as Lear finds "reason in madness" so Gloucester learns to "see" in his blindness....The whole play is built on this double paradox.[2]

[1]"*King Lear* and the Theory of the Sight Pattern," in R. Brower and R. Poirier, eds. *In Defense of Reading* (New York: E. P. Dutton and Co., 1963), pp. 133-52.

[2]Alpers gives the references for the elements of his quotation as follows: J. I. M.

But when Alpers looks to the text for evidence for this theory he discovers that there is none. Acts of vision and references to eyes are notably present, but their function is not to symbolize moral insight; rather, they insist upon the ordinary, literal uses of eyes: to express feeling, to weep, and to recognize others. Unquestionably there is truth in this. But the evidence for Alpers' view is not perfectly clear and his concepts are not accurately explored in terms of the events of the play. The acts of vision named in the lines he cites are those of giving *looks* and of *staring*, and the function of these acts is exactly *not* to express feeling, or else to express cruel feeling. Why? Because the power of the eyes to see is being used in isolation from their capacity to weep, which seems the most literal use of them to express feeling.

Alper's dominant insistence upon the third ordinary use of the eyes, their role in recognizing others, counters common readings of the two moments of recognition central to the "sight pattern": Gloucester's recognition of Edgar's innocence and Lear's recognition of Cordelia. "The crucial issue is not insight, but recognition" (Alpers, p. 149): Gloucester is not enabled to "see" because he is blinded, the truth is heaped upon him from Regan's luxuriant cruelty; Cordelia need not be viewed symbolically, the infinite poignance of her reconciliation with Lear is sufficiently accounted for by his literal recognition of her. — But then it becomes incomprehensible why or how these children have *not* been recognized by these parents; they had not become literally invisible. They are in each case banished, disowned, sent out of sight. And the question remains: What makes it possible for them to be *received* again?

In each case, there is a condition necessary in order that the recognition take place: Gloucester and Lear must each first recognize himself, and allow himself to be recognized, revealed to another. In Gloucester, the recognition comes at once, on hearing Regan's news:

> O my follies! Then Edgar was abused.
> Kind Gods, forgive me that, and prosper him!
>
> (III. vii. 90-91)

Stewart, *Character and Motive in Shakespeare* (New York: Longmans, Green and Co., 1949), pp. 20-21; R. B. Heilman, *This Great Stage* (Baton Rouge: Louisiana State University Press, 1948), p. 25; L. C. Knights, *Some Shakespearean Themes* (London: Chatto and Windus, 1959), p. 107; *King Lear,* ed. K. Muir (Cambridge: Harvard University Press, 1952, Arden edition), lx.

In each of these two lines he puts his recognition of himself first. Lear's self-revelation comes harder, but when it comes it has the same form:

> Do not laugh at me;
> For, as I am a man, I think this lady
> To be my child Cordelia.   (IV. vii. 68-70)

He refers to himself three times, then "my child" recognizes her simultaneously with revealing himself (as her father). Self-recognition is, phenomenologically, a form of insight; and it is because of its necessity in recognizing others that critics have felt its presence here.[3]

Lear does not attain his insight until the end of the fourth Act, and when he does it is climactic. This suggests that Lear's dominating motivation to this point, from the time things go wrong in the opening scene, is *to avoid being recognized.* The isolation and avoidance of eyes is what the obsessive sight imagery of the play underlines. This is the clue I want to follow first in reading out the play.

If the blinding is unnecessary for Gloucester's true seeing of Edgar, why is Gloucester blinded? Alpers' suggestion, in line with his emphasis on the literal presence of eyes, is that because the eyes are physically the most precious and most vulnerable of human organs, the physical assault on them best dramatizes man's capacity for cruelty. But if the symbolic interpretation seems hysterical, this explanation seems overcasual, and in any case does not follow the words. Critics who have looked for a *meaning* in the blinding have been looking for the right thing. But they have been looking for an aesthetic meaning or justification; looking too high, as it were. It is aesthetically justified (it is "not an irrelevant horror" (Muir, p. lx)) just because it is morally, spiritually justified, in a way which directly relates the eyes to their power to see.

---

[3]This of course is not to say that such critics have correctly interpreted this feeling of insight, and it does not touch Alpers' claim that such critics have in particular interpreted "moral insight" as "the perception of moral truths"; nor, finally does it weaken Alpers' view of such an interpretation as moralizing, hence evading, the significance of (this) tragedy. I am not, that is, regarding Alpers and the critics with whom, on this point, he is at odds, as providing alternative readings of the play, between which I am choosing or adjudicating. Their relation is more complex. Another way of seeing this is to recognize that Alpers does not deny the presence of a controlling "sight pattern" in *King Lear,* but he transforms the significance of this pattern.

> *Glou.*   ...but I shall see
>   The winged vengeance overtake such children.
> *Corn.* See't shalt thou never.... (III. vii. 64-66)

And then Cornwall puts out one of Gloucester's eyes. A servant inter-
poses, wounding Cornwall; then Regan stabs the servant from behind, and his dying words, meant to console or establish connection
with Gloucester, ironically recall Cornwall to his interrupted work:

> *First Serv.* O! I am slain. My Lord, you have one eye left
>   To see some mischief on him. Oh! *(Dies.)*
> *Corn.* Lest it see more, prevent it. Out, vile jelly!
>   (III. vii. 80-82)

Of course the idea of punishment by plucking out eyes has been im-
planted earlier, by Lear and by Goneril and most recently by Gloucester himself, and their suggestions implicate all of them spiritually
in Cornwall's deed. But Cornwall himself twice gives the immediate
cause of his deed, once for each eye: to prevent Gloucester from
seeing, and in particular to prevent him from seeing *him*. That this
scene embodies the most open expression of cruelty is true enough;
and true that it suggests the limitlessness of cruelty, once it is given
its way—that it will find its way to the most precious objects. It is
also true that the scene is symbolic, but what it symbolizes is a function of what it means. The physical cruelty symbolizes (or instances)
the psychic cruelty which pervades the play; but what this particular
act of cruelty means is that cruelty cannot bear to be seen. It literalizes
evil's ancient love of darkness.

This relates the blinding to Cornwall's needs; but it is also related
to necessities of Gloucester's character. It has an aptness which takes
on symbolic value, the horrible aptness of retribution. (It is not
merely literary critics who look for meaning in suffering, attempting
to rationalize it. Civilizations have always done it, in their myths and
laws; men do it in their dreams and fears of vengeance. They learned
to do it from Gods.) For Gloucester has a fault, not particularly
egregious, in fact common as dirt, but in a tragic accumulation in
which society disgorges itself upon itself, it shows clearly enough;
and I cannot understand his immediate and complete acquiescence
in the fate which has befallen him (his acknowledgment of his folly,
his acceptance of Edgar's innocence, and his wish for forgiveness all
take just twenty syllables) without supposing that it strikes him as a

retribution, forcing him to an insight about his life as a whole. Not, however, necessarily a true insight. He has revealed his fault in the opening speeches of the play, in which he tells Kent of his *shame*. (That shame is the subject of those speeches is emphasized by Coleridge; but he concentrates, appropriately enough, on *Edmund's* shame.) He says that now he is "braz'd to it," that is, used to admitting that he has fathered a bastard, and also perhaps carrying the original sense of soldered fast to it. He recognizes the moral claim upon himself, as he says twice, to "acknowledge" his bastard; but all this means to him is that he acknowledge that he has a bastard for a son. He does not acknowledge *him*, as a son or a person, with *his* feelings of illegitimacy and being cast out. *That* is something Gloucester ought to be ashamed of; his shame is itself more shameful than his one piece of licentiousness. This is one of the inconveniences of shame, that it is generally inaccurate, attaches to the wrong thing. ...

That Gloucester still feels shame about his son is shown not just by his descriptions of himself, but also by the fact that Edmund "...hath been out nine years, and away he shall again" (I. i. 32), and by the fact that Gloucester has to joke about him: joking is a familiar specific for brazening out shame, calling enlarged attention to the thing you do not want naturally noticed. (Hence the comedian sports disfigurement.) But if the failure to recognize others is a failure to let others recognize you, a fear of what is revealed to them, an avoidance of their eyes, then it is exactly shame which is the cause of his withholding of recognition. (It is not simply his legal treatment that Edmund is railing against.) For shame is the specific discomfort produced by the sense of being looked at, the avoidance of the sight of others is the reflex it produces. Guilt is different; there the reflex is to avoid discovery. As long as no one *knows* what you have done, you are safe; or your conscience will press you to confess it and accept punishment. Under shame, what must be covered up is not your deed, but yourself. It is a more primitive emotion than guilt, as inescapable as the possession of a body, the first object of shame. — Gloucester suffers the same punishment he inflicts: in his respectability, he avoided eyes; when respectability falls away and the disreputable come into power, his eyes are avoided. In the fear of Gloucester's poor eyes there is the promise that cruelty can be overcome, and instruction about how it can be overcome. That is the content which justifies the scene of his blinding, aesthetically, psychologically, morally.

This raises again the question of the relation between the Gloucester sub-plot and the Lear plot. The traditional views seem on the whole to take one of two lines: Gloucester's fate parallels Lear's in order that it become more universal (because Gloucester is an ordinary man, not a distant King, or because in happening to more than one it may happen to any); or more concrete (since Gloucester suffers physically what Lear suffers psychically). Such suggestions are not wrong, but they leave out of account the specific climactic moment at which the sub-plot surfaces and Lear and Gloucester face one another.

> *Edgar.* I would not take this from report; it is,
> And my heart breaks at it. (IV. vi. 142-143)

I have felt that, but more particularly I have felt an obscurer terror at this moment than at any other in the play. The considerations so far introduced begin, I think, to explain the source of that feeling.

Two questions immediately arise about that confrontation: (1) This is the scene in which Lear's madness is first broken through; in the next scene he is reassembling his sanity. Both the breaking through and the reassembling are manifested by his *recognizing* someone, and my first question is: Why is it Gloucester whom Lear is first able to recognize from his madness, and in recognizing whom his sanity begins to return? (2) *What* does Lear see when he recognizes Gloucester? What is he confronted by?

1. Given our notion that recognizing a person depends upon allowing oneself to be recognized by him, the question becomes: Why is it Gloucester whose recognition Lear is first able to bear? The obvious answer is: Because Gloucester is blind. Therefore one can be, can only be, *recognized by him without being seen,* without having to bear eyes upon oneself.

Leading up to Lear's acknowledgment ("I know thee well enough …") there is that insane flight of exchanges about Gloucester's eyes; it is the only active cruelty given to Lear by Shakespeare, apart from his behavior in the abdication scene. But here it seems uncaused, deliberate cruelty inflicted for its own sake upon Gloucester's eyes.

> *Glou.* Dost thou know me?
> *Lear.* I remember thine eyes well enough. Dost thou squiny at me?
>   No, do thy worst, blind Cupid; I'll not love.
>   Read thou this challenge; mark but the penning of it.
>   (IV. vi. 137-140)

(This last line, by the way, and Gloucester's response to it, seems a clear enough reference to Gloucester's reading of Edmund's letter, carrying here the suggestion that he was blind then.)

> *Glou.* Were all thy letters suns [sons?] , I could not see.
> *Lear.* Read.
> *Glou.* What! with the case of eyes?
> *Lear.* Oh, ho! are you there with me? No eyes in your head, nor no money in your purse? Your eyes are in a heavy case, your purse in a light: yet you see how this world goes.
> *Glou.* I see it feelingly.
> *Lear.* What! art mad? A man may see how this world goes with no eyes. . . .

*   *   *

> Get thee glass eyes;
> And, like a scurvy politician, seem
> To see the things thou dost not. . . .   (IV. vi. 141-151; 172-174)

Lear is picking at Gloucester's eyes, as if to make sure they are really gone. When he is sure, he recognizes him:

> If thou wilt weep my fortunes, take my eyes;
> I know thee well enough; thy name is Gloucester. . . .
>   (IV. vi. 178-179)

(Here "take my eyes" can be read as a crazy consolation: your eyes wouldn't have done you any good anyway in this case; you would need to see what I have seen to weep my fortunes; I would give up my eyes not to have seen it.)

This picking spiritually relates Lear to Cornwall's and Regan's act in first blinding Gloucester, for Lear does what he does for the same reason they do—in order not to be seen by this man, whom he has brought harm. (Lear exits from this scene running. From what? From "A Gentleman, with Attendants." His first words to them are: "No rescue? What! A prisoner?" But those questions had interrupted the Gentleman's opening words to him, "Your most dear daughter —". Lear runs not because in his madness he cannot distinguish friends from enemies but because he knows that recognition of himself is imminent. Even madness is no rescue.)

2. This leads to the second question about the scene: What is Lear confronted by in acknowledging Gloucester? It is easy to say: Lear is confronted here with the direct consequences of his conduct, of his covering up in rage and madness, of his having given up authority and kingdom for the wrong motives, to the wrong people; and he is for the first time confronting himself. What is difficult is

to show that this is not merely or vaguely symbolic, and that it is not merely an access of knowledge which Lear undergoes. Gloucester has by now become not just a figure "parallel" to Lear, but Lear's double; he does not merely represent Lear, but is psychically identical with him. So that what comes to the surface in this meeting is not a related story, but Lear's submerged mind. This, it seems to me, is what gives the scene its particular terror, and gives to the characters what neither could have alone. In this fusion of plots and identities, we have the great image, the double or mirror image, of everyman who has gone to every length to avoid himself, caught at the moment of coming upon himself face to face. (Against this, "take my eyes" strikes psychotic power.)

The identity is established at the end of the blinding scene, by Regan:

> Go thrust him out at gates, and let him smell
> His way to Dover. (III. vii. 92-93)

It is by now commonly appreciated that Gloucester had, when that scene began, no plans for going to Dover. Interpreters have accounted for this discrepancy by suggesting that Shakespeare simply wanted all his characters present at Dover for the climax, adding that the repeated question "Wherefore to Dover?" may have put that destination in Gloucester's mind, which has been kicked out of shape. But this interprets the wrong thing, for it overlooks the more obvious, anyway the first, discrepancy. The question is why *Regan* assumes that he is going to Dover. (Her husband, for example, does not: "Turn out that eyeless villain.") We may wish here to appeal to those drummed "Dover's" to explain her mind, and to suppose that she associates that name with the gathering of all her enemies. But the essential fact is that the name is primarily caught to the image of her father. In her mind, the man she is sending on his way to Dover is the man she *knows* is sent on his way to Dover: in her paroxysms of cruelty, she imagines that she has just participated in blinding her father.

And Gloucester apparently thinks so too, for he then, otherwise inexplicably, sets out for Dover. "Otherwise inexplicably": for it is *no* explanation to say that "the case-histories of suicides contain stranger obsessive characteristics than this" (Muir, xlix). There is no reason, at this stage—other than our cultural advantage in having read the play before—to assume that Gloucester is planning suicide. He sets out for Dover because he is *sent* there: by himself, in sending

Lear, in whose identity he is now submerged; and by the thrust of
Regan's evil and confusion. But he has no *reason* to go there, not
even some inexplicable wish to commit suicide there. At the beginning of the plan to go to Dover he says "I have no way" (IV. i. 18).
It is only at the end of that scene that he mentions Dover *cliff* (IV.
i. 73). One can, of course, explain that he had been thinking of the
cliff all along. But what the text suggests is that, rather than taking
a plan for suicide as our explanation for his insistence on using
Dover cliff, we ought to see his thought of the cliff, and consequently
of suicide, as *his* explanation of his otherwise mysterious mission to
Dover. Better suicide than no reason at all.

When Shakespeare's lapses in plot construction are noticed, critics
who know that he is nevertheless the greatest of the bards under-
take to excuse him, or to justify the lapse by the great beauty of
its surroundings. A familiar excuse is that the lapse will in any case
not be noticed in performance. No doubt there are lapses of this
kind, and no doubt they can sometimes be covered by such excuses.
But it ought also to occur to us that what looks like a lapse is sometimes meant, and that our failure to notice the lapse is just that,
our failure. This is what has happened to us in the present scene.
We "do not notice" Regan's confusion of identity because we share
it, and in failing to understand Gloucester's blanked condition (or
rather, in insisting upon understanding it from our point of view)
we are doing what the characters in the play are seen to do: we avoid
him. And so we are implicated in the failures we are witnessing, we
share the responsibility for tragedy.

This is further confirmed in another outstanding lapse, or crux
—Gloucester's appearance, led by an old man, to Edgar-Tom. The
question, as generally asked, is: Why does Edgar wait, on seeing his
father blind, and hearing that his father knows his mistake, before
revealing himself to him? The answers which suggest themselves to
that question are sophisticated, not the thing itself. For example:
Edgar wants to clear himself in the eyes of the world before revealing
himself. (But he could still let his *father* know. Anyway, he does tell
his father before he goes to challenge Edmund.) Edgar "wants to
impose a penance on his father, and to guarantee the genuineness
and permanence of the repentance" (Muir, l). (This seems to me psychologically fantastic; it suggests that the first thing which occurs to
Edgar on seeing his father blinded is to exact some further punishment. Or else it makes Edgar into a monster of righteousness; where-
as he is merely self-righteous.) Edgar wants to cure his father of his

desire to commit suicide. (But *revealing himself* would seem the surest and most immediate way to do that.) And so on. My dissatisfaction with these answers is not that they are psychological explanations, but that they are explanations of the wrong thing, produced by the wrong question: Why does Edgar *delay*? "Delay" implies he is going to later. But we do not *know* (at this stage) that he will; we do not so much as know that he intends to. In terms of our reading of the play so far, we are alerted to the fact that what Edgar does is most directly described as *avoiding recognition. That* is what we want an explanation for.

And first, this action bears the same meaning, or has the same consequences, it always has in this play: mutilating cruelty. This is explicit in one of Gloucester's first utterances after the blinding, led into Edgar's presence:

> Oh! dear son Edgar,
> The food of thy abused father's wrath;
> Might I but live to see thee in my touch,
> I'd say I had eyes again. (IV. i. 21-24)

So Edgar's avoidance of Gloucester's recognition precisely deprives Gloucester of his eyes again. This links him, as Lear was and will be linked, to Cornwall and the sphere of open evil.

This reading also has consequences for our experience of two subsequent events of the play.

1. In a play in which, as has often been said, each of the characters is either very good or very bad, this revelation of Edgar's capacity for cruelty—and the *same* cruelty as that of the evil characters—shows how radically implicated good is in evil; in a play of disguises, how often they are disguised. And Edgar is the ruler at the end of the play, Lear's successor, the man who must, in Albany's charge, "the gor'd state sustain." (A very equivocal charge, containing no assurance that its body may be nursed back to health; but simply nursed.) If good is to grow anywhere in this state, it must recognize, and face, its continuity with, its location within a maze of evil. Edgar's is the most Christian sensibility in the play, as Edmund's is the most Machiavellian. If the Machiavellian fails in the end, he very nearly succeeds; and if the Christian succeeds, his success is deeply compromised.

2. To hold to the fact that Edgar is avoiding recognition makes better sense to me of that grotesque guiding of Gloucester up no hill to no cliff to no suicide than any other account I know. The special

quality of this scene, with its purest outbreak of grotesquerie, has been recognized at least since Wilson Knight's essay of 1930.[4] But to regard it as *symbolic* of the play's emphasis on the grotesque misses what makes it so grotesque, and fails to account for the fact that Edgar and Gloucester find themselves in this condition. It is grotesque because it is so *literal* a consequence of avoiding the facts. It is not the emblem of the Lear universe, but an instance of what has led its minds to their present state: there are no lengths to which we may not go in order to avoid being revealed, even to those we love and are loved by. Or rather, especially to those we love and are loved by: to other people it is *easy* not to be known. That grotesque walk is not full of promise for our lives. It is not, for example, a picture of mankind making its way up Purgatory;[5] for Gloucester's character is not purified by it, but extirpated. It shows what people will *have* to say and try to mean to one another when they are incapable of acknowledging to one another what they have to acknowledge. To fill this scene with nourishing, profound meaning is to see it from Edgar's point of view; that is, to avoid what is there. Edgar is Ahab, trying to harpoon the meaning of his life into something external to it; and we believe him, and serve him. He is Hedda Gabler, with her ugly demand for beauty. In the fanciful, childish deceit of his plan, he is Tom Sawyer in the last chapters of *Huckleberry Finn*, enveloping Jim's prison with symbols of escape, instead of opening the door.

If one wishes a psychological explanation for Edgar's behavior, the question to be answered is: Why does Edgar avoid his father's recognition? Two answers suggest themselves. (1) He is himself ashamed and guilty. He was as gullible as his father was to Edmund's "invention." He failed to confront his father, to trust his love, exactly as his father had failed him. He is as responsible for his father's blinding as his father is. He wants to make it up to his father before asking for his recognition—to make it up instead of repenting, acknowledging; he wants to *do* something instead of stopping and seeing. So he goes on doing the very thing which needs making up for. (2) He cannot bear the fact that his father is incapable, impotent, maimed. He wants his father still to be a father, powerful, so that *he* can remain a child. For otherwise they are simply two human beings

---

[4]"*King Lear* and the Comedy of the Grotesque," one of the studies comprising *The Wheel of Fire*, originally published by Oxford University Press, 1930; published in the fifth revised edition by Meridian Books, Inc., New York, 1957.

[5]Suggested by R. W. Chambers, *King Lear*, 1940; cited by Muir, p. 1.

in need of one another, and it is not usual for parents and children to manage that transformation, becoming for one another nothing more, but nothing less, than unaccommodated men. That is what Lear took Edgar to be, but that was a mad, ironic compliment; to become natural again, men need to do more than remove their clothes; for they can also cover up their embarrassment by nakedness. Men have their inventions, their accommodations.

We learn in the course of Edgar's tale, after his successful duel with Edmund, when it was that he brought himself to allow his father to recognize him:

> Never—O fault!—revealed myself unto him
> Until some half-hour past, when I was arm'd. ...
>
> (V. iii. 192-193)

Armed, and with the old man all but seeped away, he feels safe enough to give his father vision again and bear his recognition. As sons fear, and half wish, it is fatal. Now he will never know whether, had he challenged recognition when recognition was denied, at home, both of them could have survived it. That Edgar is so close to the thing love demands contributes to the grotesque air of the late scenes with his father.[6] Love does maintain itself under betrayal; it does allow, and forward, its object's wish to find the edge of its own existence; it does not shrink from recognition that its object is headed for, or has survived, radical change, with its attendant destructions—which is the way love knows that a betrayal is ended, and is why it provides the context for new innocence. But Edgar does not know that love which has such power also has the power to kill, and, in going to the lengths he takes it, must be capable of absolute scrupulousness. It cannot lead, it can only accompany, past the point it has been, and it must feel that point. It is Edgar's self-assurance here which mocks his Christian thoroughness.

We now have elements with which to begin an analysis of the most controversial of the *Lear* problems, the nature of Lear's motivation in his opening (abdication) scene. The usual interpretations follow one of three main lines: Lear is senile; Lear is puerile; Lear is not to be understood in natural terms, for the whole scene has a fairy tale or ritualistic character which simply must be accepted as the premise from which the tragedy is derived. Arguments ensue, in

[6]The passage from this sentence to the end of the paragraph was added as the result of a conversation with Rose Mary Harbison.

each case, about whether Shakespeare is justified in what he is asking his audience to accept. My hypothesis will be that Lear's behavior in this scene is explained by — the tragedy begins because of —
the same motivation which manipulates the tragedy throughout its
course, from the scene which precedes the abdication, through the
storm, blinding, evaded reconciliations, to the final moments: by
the attempt to avoid recognition, the shame of exposure, the threat
of self-revelation. ...

We imagine that Lear *must* be wildly abused (blind, puerile,
and the rest) because the thing works out so badly. But it doesn't
begin badly, and it is far from incomprehensible conduct. It is, in
fact, quite ordinary. A parent is bribing love out of his children; two
of them accept the bribe, and despise him for it; the third shrinks
from the attempt, as though from violation. Only this is a king, this
bribe is the last he will be able to offer; everything in his life, and in
the life of his state, depends upon its success. We need not assume
that he does not know his two older daughters, and that they are
giving him false coin in return for his real bribes, though perhaps
like most parents he is willing not to notice it. But more than this:
there is reason to assume that the open possibility — or the open fact
— that they are *not* offering true love is exactly what he wants. Trouble
breaks out only with Cordelia's "Nothing," and her broken resolution to be silent. — What does he want, and what is the meaning of
the trouble which then breaks out?

Go back to the confrontation scene with Gloucester:

> If thou wilt weep my fortunes, take my eyes.

The obvious rhetoric of those words is that of an appeal, or a bargain. But it is also warning, and a command: If you weep for me, the
same thing will happen to me that happened to you; do not let me
see what you are weeping for. Given the whole scene, with its con-
centrated efforts at warding off Gloucester, that line says explicitly
what it is Lear is warding off: Gloucester's sympathy, his love. And
earlier:

> *Glou.* O! Let me kiss that hand.
> *Lear.* Let me wipe it first, it smells of mortality.

(IV. vi. 134-135)

Mortality, the hand without rings of power on it, cannot be lovable.
He feels unworthy of love when the reality of lost power comes over
him. That is what his plan was to have avoided by exchanging his

fortune for his love at one swap. He cannot bear love when he has no
reason to be loved, perhaps because of the helplessness, the passive-
ness which that implies, which some take for impotence. And he
wards it off for the reason for which people do ward off being loved,
because it presents itself to them as a demand:

> *Lear.* No. Do thy worst, blind Cupid; I'll not love.
>
> (IV. vi. 139)

Gloucester's presence strikes Lear as the demand for love; he knows
he is being offered love; he tries to deny the offer by imagining that
he has been solicited (this is the relevance of "blind Cupid" as the
sign of a brothel); and he doesn't want to pay for it, for he may get it,
and may not, and either is intolerable. Besides, he has recently done
just that, paid his all for love. The long fantasy of his which precedes
this line ("Let copulation thrive".... "There is the sulphurous
pit—burning, scalding, stench, consumption...") contains his most
sustained expression of disgust with sexuality (ll. ii. 6ff.)—as though
furiously telling himself that what was wrong with his plan was not
the debasement of love his bargain entailed, but the fact that love
itself is inherently debased and so unworthy from the beginning of
the bargain he had made for it. That is a maddening thought; but
still more comforting than the truth. For some spirits, to be loved
knowing you cannot return that love, is the most radical of psychic
tortures.

This is the way I understand that opening scene with the three
daughters. Lear knows it is a bribe he offers, and—part of him anyway—wants exactly what a bribe can buy: (1) false love; and (2) a
public expression of love. That is: he wants something he does not
have to return *in kind*, something which a division of his property
fully pays for. And he wants to *look* like a loved man—for the sake
of the subjects, as it were. He is perfectly happy with his little plan,
until Cordelia speaks. Happy not because he is blind, but because he
is getting what he wants, his plan is working. Cordelia is alarming
precisely because he *knows* she is offering the real thing, offering
something a more opulent third of his kingdom cannot, must not,
repay; putting a claim upon him he cannot face. She threatens to
expose both his plan for returning false love with no love, and expose the necessity for that plan—his terror of being loved, of need-
ing love. ...

The final scene opens with Lear and Cordelia repeating or completing their actions in their opening scene; again Lear abdicates, and again Cordelia loves and is silent. ... Lear's opening speech of this final scene is not the correction but the repetition of his strategy in the first scene, or a new tactic designed to win the old game; and it is equally disastrous.

> *Cord.* Shall we not see these daughters and these sisters?
> *Lear.* No, no, no, no!...   (V. iii. 7-8)

He cannot finally face the thing he has done; and this means what it always does, that he cannot bear being seen. He is anxious to go off to prison, with Cordelia; his love now is in the open—that much circumstance has done for him; but it remains imperative that it be confined, out of sight. (Neither Lear nor Cordelia, presumably, knows that the soldier in command is Gloucester's son; they feel unknown.) He is still ashamed, and the fantasy expressed in this speech ("We two alone will sing like birds i' the cage") is the same fantasy he brings on the stage with him in the first scene, the thwarting of which causes his maddened destructiveness. There Cordelia had offered him the marriage pledge ("Obey you, love you, and most honor you"), and she has shared his fantasy fully enough to wish to heal political strife with a kiss (or perhaps it is just the commonest fantasy of women):

> *Cord.*   Restoration hang
> Thy medicine on my lips. ...   (IV. vii. 26-27)

(But after such abdication, what restoration? The next time we hear the words "hang" and "medicine," they announce death.) This gesture is as fabulous as anything in the opening scene. Now, at the end, Lear returns her pledge with his lover's song, his invitation to voyage ("...so we'll live, and pray, and sing, and tell old tales, and laugh..."). The fantasy of this speech is as full of detail as a day dream, and it is clearly a happy dream for Lear. He has found at the end a way to have what he has wanted from the beginning. His tone is not: we will love *even though* we are in prison; but: because we are hidden together we can love. He has come to accept his love, not by making room in the world for it, but by denying its relevance to the world. He does not renounce the world in going to prison, but flees from it, to earthly pleasure. The astonishing image of "God's spies" (V. iii. 17) stays beyond me, but in part it contains the final emphasis upon looking without being seen; and it cites an intimacy which requires no reciprocity with real men. Like Gloucester toward Dover, Lear anticipates God's call. He is not experiencing reconciliation with a daughter, but partnership in a mystic marriage.

If so, it cannot be, as is often suggested, that when he says

> Upon such sacrifices, my Cordelia,
> The Gods themselves throw incense. (V. iii. 20-21)

he is thinking simply of going to prison with Cordelia as a sacrifice. It seems rather that, the lines coming immediately after his love song, it is their love itself which has the meaning of sacrifice. As though the ideas of love and of death are interlocked in his mind — and in particular of death as a payment or placation for the granting of love. His own death, because acknowledging love still presents itself to him as an annihilation of himself. And her death, because now that he admits her love, he must admit, what he knew from the beginning, that he is impotent to sustain it. This is the other of Cordelia's sacrifices — of love to secrecy. ...

It can be said that what Lear is ashamed of is not his need for love and his inability to return it, but of the *nature* of his love for Cordelia. It is too far from plain love of father for daughter. Even if we resist seeing in it the love of lovers, it is at least incompatible with the idea of her having any (other) lover. There is a moment, beyond the words, when this comes to the surface of the action. It is the moment Lear is waking from his madness, no longer incapable of seeing the world, but still not strong enough to protect his thoughts: "Methinks I should know you and know this man ..." (IV. vii. 64). I take it "this man" is generally felt to refer to Kent (disguised as Caius), for there is clearly no reason to suppose Lear knows the Doctor, the only other man present. Certainly this is plausible; but in fact Lear never does acknowledge Kent, as he does his child Cordelia.[7] And after this recognition he goes on to ask, "Am I in France?"

---

[7]Professor Jonas Barish — to whom I am indebted for other suggestions about this essay as well as the present one — has pointed out to me that in my eagerness to solve all the *King Lear* problems I have neglected trying an account of Kent's plan in delaying making himself known ("Yet to be known shortens my made intent" (IV. vii. 9)). This omission is particularly important because Kent's is the one delay that causes no harm to others, hence it provides an internal measure of those harms. I do not understand his "dear cause" (IV. iii. 52), but I think the specialness of Kent's delay has to do with these facts: (1) It never prevents his perfect faithfulness to his duties of service; these do not require — Kent does not permit them to require — personal recognition in order to be performed. This sense of the finitude of the demands placed upon Kent, hence of the harm and of the good he can perform, is

This question irresistibly (to me) suggests that the man he thinks he should know is the man he expects to be with his daughter, her husband. This would be unmistakable if he directs his "this man" to the Doctor, taking him for, but not able to make him out as, France. He finds out it is not, and the next time we see him he is pressing off to prison with his child, and there is no further thought of her husband. It is a standing complaint that Shakespeare's explanation of France's absence is perfunctory. It is more puzzling that Lear himself never refers to him, not even when he is depriving him of her forever. Either France has ceased to exist for Lear, or it is importantly from him that he wishes to reach the shelter of prison.

I do not wish to suggest that "avoidance of love" and "avoidance of a particular kind of love" are alternative hypotheses about this play. On the contrary, they seem to me to interpret one another. Avoidance of love is always, or always begins as, an avoidance of a particular kind of love: men do not just naturally not love, they learn not to. And our lives begin by having to accept under the name of love whatever closeness is offered, and by then having to forgo its object. And the avoidance of a particular love, or the acceptance of it, will spread to every other; every love, in acceptance or rejection, is mirrored in every other. It is part of the miracle of the vision in *King Lear* to bring this before us, so that we do not care whether the *kind* of love felt between these two is forbidden according to man's lights. We care

a function of his complete absorption into his social office, in turn a function of his being the only principal character in the play (apart from the Fool) who does not appear as the member of a *family*. (2) He does not delay revealing himself to Cordelia, only (presumably) to Lear. A reason for that would be that since the King has banished him it is up to the King to reinstate him; he will not presume on his old rank. (3) If his plan goes beyond finding some way, or just waiting, for Lear to recognize him first (not out of pride but out of right) then perhaps it is made irrelevant by finding Lear again only in his terminal state, or perhaps it always consisted only in doing what he tries to do there, find an opportunity to tell Lear about Caius and ask for pardon. It may be wondered that we do not feel Lear's fragmentary recognitions of Kent to leave something undone, nor Kent's hopeless attempts to hold Lear's attention to be crude intrusions, but rather to amplify a sadness already amplified past sensing. This may be accounted for partly by Kent's pure expression of the special poignance of the servant's office, requiring a life centered in another life, exhausted in loyalty and in silent witnessing (a silence Kent broke and Lear must mend); partly by the fact that Cordelia has fully recognized him: "To be acknowledg'd, Madam, is o'er-paid" (IV. vii. 4); partly by the fact that when his master Lear is dead, it is his master who calls him, and his last words are those of obedience.

whether love is or is not altogether forbidden to man, whether we may not altogether be incapable of it, of admitting it into our world. We wonder whether we may always go mad between the equal efforts and terrors at once of rejecting and of accepting love.

Lear's Theatre Poetry

by Marvin Rosenberg

Of course *Lear* can be staged. It has been, and will continue to be. Criticism's only sane posture, in fact, is to insist that it must be staged, if the full dimensions of Shakespeare's art are to be perceived sensually as well as cognitively, as the playwright intended.

The staging is not easy. The scenic demands are considerable; the demands on the actor ultimate. Not a single character can be conveniently synthesized into a type: each is designed as a polyphony, to use Mikhoels' word, each is made of mixed and even contradictory qualities. Lear most of all; we have seen that the fissioning of his opposing attributes almost bursts the limits of character possibility. He is all the four streams—and all the tributaries—of characterization we followed: titan king, tough king, mad king, everyman king. These four were only singled out for the convenience of discussion, because they seemed to dominate actors' conceptions: something of all of them—and more—informed such distinguished performances as by Scofield, Devrient, Salvini, Carnovsky, Gielgud. Similarly, the conflicting impulses, ideas, and even physical acts of Lear must, like the play itself, back-forth in tidal flow; to deny the dialectic to the character on the stage—or in criticism—is to congeal the whole mighty ocean of the play. This form, as much as what the play says and does, contributes to its power continuously to arouse.

The temptation to congeal, simplify, fit all into an easily graspable pattern, is great; particularly with the lesser characters. But they too are constellations—Redgrave's word; we have seen how multiple, countering motivations and qualities shape their designs: the best are somewhere discolored, the worst show moldings of dignity and understandable motivation.

To resist closure, to keep the dialectic of the characters—and the play—open-ended, is hard enough for the imagining mind; harder in the theatre where the dynamic designs must be enclosed in physical shapes. But only in the theatre, for the same reason, can the whole be realized. Actors can meet the challenge: can, with their faces and bodies, project the play's ambiguities (as these ambiguities may be intuited by them, or made present to them by scholar-critics). Shakespeare counted on this: hence so much of *Lear*'s language is non-verbal, designed for the actor's face and body rather than his tongue. Often, at crucial points, the play's meaning depends on subtextual gesture that may deny, undercut, play against the words. Thus, to recapitulate, Lear's furious angers may issue from a body partly aching for love. The ambivalence of Edgar's curious treatment of Gloster must have, to make sense, nuances of accompanying physical expression. Cordelia's inner resistances are barely indicated in words, are meaningful only in terms of a *persona* projecting them. This of course is why so many arguments flower over these and the other character designs: because so much has to be said without words, and what that is must be intuited. The art of the great actor, as Shakespeare knew, is to say these things superbly, even when, with face and body, as with the words, more than one thing must be said at a time.

What Shakespeare says with faces and bodies—and things—involves a special kind of poetry. Sometimes *Lear's* physical language matches the verbal, as where bodies are wrenched and pierced. Sometimes the physical must say what the words suggest: as when Lear, Fool, Kent, Edgar, Gloster must indicate as a continuing background through Act III the intense cold, the acute bodily discomfort, of heath and hovel. But beyond this, *Lear*'s language of gesture has a cumulative symbolic content and texture that command the eye and mind to a special poetic experience as subtle and deeply stirring in its way as the ear-mind's experience of the words (though of course the two complement each other, cannot be separated except for discussion). The whole of this fluid tapestry can be made present only to the seeing eye; the reading mind cannot encompass it. The past pages have traced the artistry of *Lear*'s visual imagery; I will summarize here, building on my definition of dramatic poetry:

> an organic structure of verbal symbols, with associated sounds, rich in denotative detail and connotative reverberation and ambiguity, often presented in recurrent, rhythmic patterns and changing per-

spectives that accumulate and extend the power of the whole to stimulate feeling, thought, and kinesthetic response in its audience.

How does this definition apply to *Lear*'s visual imagery (in association with its imagery of sound: the non-verbal poetry of cries, howls, barks, trumpets and other music)? The best way to approach Shakespeare's composition of spectacle is for us to imagine the play as a mime with linked non-verbal sounds. This will enable us to discern, in relief, the poem of Shakespeare's gestures.

For an easy bridge to this imagining, I will concentrate on a single motif in the *Lear* language: the familiar motif of seeing. We have followed the orchestration of the idea through the network of such words as *see, sight, blindness, look, looking glass,* and have sensed the growing reverberative implications for perception, understanding, insight, knowing, and their opposites. These implications converge in Gloster's focal speech

> I see it feelingly.   (150)

On one level, the blind man actually reaches out to Lear, and so sees him in his touch. But Gloster's way of seeing, as well as his words, suggests that he feels he has insight, he understands what is not visible, he does so with his feelings, and he does so very well. A further shadow persists—Gloster does not, even inwardly, really see well. The words say some of this but here as elsewhere words fail in *Lear;* and sight-sound imagery must complete the communication, especially when latent, subconscious impulses must be conveyed.

The scene resonates with visual, as well as verbal, echoes. Shakespeare created a string of "speaking pictures," every line and shape of which said something to the mind. We in this century are learning to demonstrate experimentally what visual artists like Shakespeare have always understood: that the eye thinks, it selects what things or what parts of things it will see, and brings to their interpretation a tremendous store of funded information and preconception. The hieroglyph, the pictograph, in our day the cartoon, more relevantly the Elizabethan emblem are examples of single visual symbolic structures that carry implications far beyond their components. The very components are eloquent. A simple straight line implies one thing; torture the line, and it says something else. Once figures become representational, as in Shakespeare's work they are, they are burdened with social meaning. Some attempts have been made to reduce Shakespeare's speaking pictures to the terms of contemporary emblems; but as an artist he was always breaking and restructuring the familiar. Thus he provided many royal tableaux, but even in the histories they were visually tensed and discolored with ambiguities of character and situation. More: as he shifted perspectives with his startling visual designs, he also used these images—as he used verbal images—in rhythmic and recurrent patterns. The images changed in light, line, color, and shape, their implications and ambiguities widened as the plays progressed. Thus, in our *Lear* mime, the first royal tableau will be refracted in succeeding images that hollow, mock, and grotesquely invert the initial experience.

Let us return to the specific visualized act of seeing. In our life, the act is so central to our way of knowing our world, and particularly the people in it, that any theatre representation is charged with allusion. Shakespeare exploited the act from his very first plays. Even in *Comedy of Errors*, many "see" words and acts help centrally to complicate and solve the puzzle of mistaken identity. In later plays, as deception grows inward, and more inward, words of seeing and insight are more subtly mated and polarized, and associated with visual images that confuse reality and appearance. The "ocular proof" Iago promises is meant to deceive. Macbeth's speech to the knife is loaded with *see* words—he believes the knife is there because he *sees* it—but it is not there.

On the stage, the simple act of looking may be powerfully dramatic. For one character to lock eyes with another, or avoid this, in silence or in speech, may be rich in ambiguity, stir deep responses. No words are needed to convey the potential of an exchange of speaking looks, as—to give an obvious example—between Edmund and Goneril. In a great actor's face the complex of feeling can converge in such singleness of passions as to be frightening; conversely, his fluid face may reveal multiple-layered, struggling impulses. For Lear to look, to see, to try to understand and identify, is peculiarly characteristic; and each seeing adds to the others, extends the implication of the visual imagery.

In the first scene this will become apparent as Lear glances at the other characters while addressing them. Here the playwright is partly, as craftsman, identifying the characters for the audience; but he is also saying something about them, and their relationship to Lear, and he is developing Lear's special way of scrutinizing those he addresses. As we observed, Lear himself has something to say about that later on: in his madness, asked if he is the king, he notes a distinguishing characteristic:

> Ay, every inch a king.
> When I do stare, see how the subject quakes.   (110-111)

At some level of his consciousness, Lear always tests, with his look, the submission of his subjects. This will be apparent, without words, in the special and different way he *looks* in the first scene at the subservient Gloster, the "fiery" Cornwall, the uncertain Albany, the masked Regan and Goneril, the withdrawn Cordelia. His act of scrutinizing will set off ripples of ambiguity in the recurrent motifs of appearance and reality, of disguise and disclosure, of the success and failure of this primary way of knowing.

In a *Lear* mime, we would observe at once a quality that, we saw, actors of Lear have sometimes accentuated in the play—the mystery of Lear's seeing—by seeming to look at the surrounding court, and all else, with an almost painful intensity, as if indeed Lear's physical capacity to see was strained—as in fact it would fail. Some actors also seemed to look beyond what they saw, as if trying to discern something not present, as if looking into another world. In the first scene, a mime audience would not need Lear's words to know that Lear will believe what he sees; and that what he sees in Goneril and Regan satisfies him. What he sees in Cordelia—however hard he looks—does not satisfy him. Then he makes a negative seeing gesture, often to be repeated—*out of my sight*. He will look elsewhere, cover his eyes, wave away what is present—if he does not like it, he will not see what is there.

On the other hand, he will be seen to communicate with what is not before him. He will look upward toward invisible powers, and seem to command them, as he would command the people around him. Here, he seems indeed to see into a world beyond reason—a vision that will be inverted ironically later.

The visual imagery of Lear's scrutiny of his world is echoed and orchestrated in mime with the disguised figures he encounters: first the banished Kent, whom he examines so closely in I, iv. Shakespeare's design of suspense, we saw, includes the possibility that Lear will recognize this disguised old friend, now called enemy, who must die if discovered: so the scrutiny functions in the action as well as the character. The seeing symbolism partly is extended by Lear's need to assure himself of his own identity, to know he is there. This is central to his confrontations with Oswald, Fool, Goneril. *Who am I sir? Dost thou call me Fool, boy? Does Lear walk thus? Speak thus?* In a mime, we would know, without speech, that Lear is looking for some assurance of who he is. It is himself he is trying to see.

Slowly Lear's way of seeing changes; the rhythm alters. When he banished Cordelia, he looked confidently to unseen powers of night and day to endorse his oath of excommunication. When he calls on the unseen to curse Goneril, he looks with appeal and his eyes are misted now; physically he cannot see so well because of tears (Shakespeare often links *eye* and *tear*), his eyes betray him, he may be seen to threaten them with plucking out; and yet on his face a new seeing is visible, that reflects, *I did her wrong*.

Charged as his glance is with anger and contempt, when he confronts Kent in the stocks, when Gloster servilely keeps him outside the castle door, he yet looks with some insecurity at the approach of Regan, and with even more when Goneril appears. His face reflects many ways of seeing at once because he is designed to experience many feelings at once. He is reduced to glancing helplessly from one to the other daughter as they beat down the number of the knights. And when next he speaks to the unseen powers, he is much less certain, his questing eyes beseech support. Again these organs of his sight cloud with tears; but we see that Lear has nevertheless begun to see reality beneath surfaces.

In the storm, he defies the invisible powers, but also defends himself against them, asks for pity—*you see me here*, he gestures—for what he sees as himself: poor, weak, despised, infirm. Raindrops join teardrops in blurring his sight; and yet a better vision becomes possible to him, the light of it shows on his face, and he kneels to pray. For a moment we see that in this dark night Lear *sees better*.

Then his eyes find Mad Tom, and he slides into madness; and the mime emphasizes a curious, ironic change that happens in his seeing. He sees things no man else sees, but he seems to see them more sharply, more craftily than he ever saw before. The whole base of his knowing, and of ours, as we experience with him, is altered—herein lies much of the power of mad scenes. Lear examines Mad Tom with the same care he gave to the scrutiny of Kent; yet he sees him in a different way. The uncertainties of the rational seeing are replaced by the certainties of the irrational. With this, values are reversed. Where before we saw that Lear saw beauty in robes and furred gowns, he now discovers it in rags and nakedness.

Before, he spoke to invisible powers he saw in space; now, mad, he speaks to invisible hallucinations he sees in space. Handy-dandy—a god or hallucination—is one any more real than the other? And behind this ambiguity lurks another: the eyes that seem to see Edgar, and then Gloster, for what they are not may, on some level, see them for what they are. The line between reason and unreason, we observed, may dissolve in cunning, or accident, or naturally. These uncertainties are latent in the text; they are made visual in Lear's looking, for instance, at Gloster in IV, vi, the face to face searching of the bloody sockets as Gloster peers sightlessly—seeingly—into Lear's eyes. What is it that the empty eyes see that shocks Lear into admitting some awareness of reality?* Silences—those punctuation marks of visual language that are often more powerful than any words or acts in the dramatic art—accent the process of Lear's mad seeing, his staring.

> Ay, every inch a king.

This is a mock king, a fool king, in a crown of weeds; one subject now, Gloster, may quake before him. When he was a real king, the subjects whom he wanted to quake did not. The stare, now, stirs ironic reverberations of the earlier unavailing look.

The mad king weeps, but the tears do not clear his sight now. Only when the great rage is stilled can he open his eyes in reason again; and then he can hardly believe what he sees. He touches Cordelia's weeping eyes, in an echo of his gesture to Gloster—eyes are for weeping, as well as seeing, whether blind or not. He must try to reestablish a base in knowing, try to see himself again, try to believe the hands he holds up before his eyes are his own.

When Cordelia is dead, he assults with his eyes—and voice—the heavens themselves; tired eyes now, tired voice, so he must assail the men who do not help him:

> Had I your tongues and eyes, I'd use them so
> That heaven's vault should crack.

The eyes are failing, for sight as well as stare, he can hardly see what to believe, cannot recognize an old friend. A dull sight.

He dies on an ambiguity. He sees something—points—(we don't need the words, *Look there, look there*) and only the visual and sub-verbal poetry sustains the action now, all else fades away. What Lear sees in Cordelia's face—vision, illusion, joy, horror, or a mixture

---

*Gloster's own failure to see is painfully visual. He does not, in fact, *see feelingly*. Without eyes, he is seen to be nearly helpless. He cannot tell the identity of his guide, though his happiness depends on it. He cannot know high ground from low, can be led anywhere, deceived anyhow. Edgar, for ambiguous purposes of his own that can only be conveyed by physical imagery, baffles Gloster's attempts to perceive reality through ears and touch. If eyes are no guarantee of seeing, neither is blindness.

of all of them—can be known *only* by what his face tell us his eyes
see. And somehow, this will be another refraction of the whole pre-
ceding, accumulating visual imagery of seeing-knowing.

Seeing involves an act. Some inanimate visual images in the play
carry a heavy load of symbolism almost by themselves. One of these
is the crown. It is hardly mentioned; and yet it is a centrally significant image in the ironic reversal in which the most powerful
are seen to be degraded, robes and furred gowns exchanged for rags,
the regal gestures once made with a royal sceptre now parodied by
a disheveled madman with a baton of straw. In the complex inter-
weaving of change and loss of garments, where fugitives disguise
themselves downward to lower station or divest themselves of opu-
lence while upstarts take on the gorgeous dress and ornaments of
higher rank, the crown is a pivotal symbol.

Lear wears it in the first scene. He might continue to wear it as
one of the "additions" to a king, and if so, with so much more irony
does he carry this ornament charged with authority, now meaningless. More likely he does not wear it again, hunting, or riding in the
night toward Regan; he dashes out into the storm, and runs
unbonneted. The next reference is to the weedy circlet he will be seen
to wear in IV, vi; but there may be other visual allusions to it. To
Mikhoels, we observed, the crown's presence was felt most in its
absence; after the first scene, when he had let it go, he would reach
up, in a habitual gesture, to reassure himself that it was there—and
it was not. So Klöpfer, in the trial scene (III, vi), took up a three-legged
copper pot, and put it upside down on his head, so that its legs simulated a crown, a simulated power image for simulated authority.
The flowered madman's crown, made of plants related to mind-
sickness, is the primary visual symbol of the irony of surface values.
Lear's gestures as he asserts his mad kingship may be exactly the
same as those he made in I, i—gestures of magnanimity, authority,
power, rage—but now they make only a grotesque charade.

The reappearance and shifting of the real crown can convey the
ambiguities of power's meaning. We followed this clearly enough
through the play, but a mime would accentuate it. Cordelia may be
seen to restore a crown to Lear in IV, vii—she is concentrating on
making him feel his royal strength again. He may be seen to wear it
in the brief passing over with the army at the beginning of Act V,
before he and Cordelia are captured. Then Edmund, their captor,
takes it, and tries it—and in this brief gesture makes visual the whole

scheme of the king's fall intersecting the bastard's rise to within one planned murder—Albany's—of a kingship. The crown will fit Edmund; but Albany will take it from him, and again a resonant symbolic visual act will be performed: Albany will try to give the crown back to Lear, but now to the true king the piece of metal is as nothing. Albany will momentarily try it himself; but being—in Edmund's Quarto speech—full of abdication and self-reproving, in a ghastly repetition of the first scene—as indeed the whole ending is visually a symbolic reprise of the assembled court at the beginning— Albany will offer to divide the crown between two rulers, Edgar and Kent. Kent will be seen to reject it, perhaps with some shock at Albany's obtuseness; Edgar will accept reluctantly the ultimate symbol of power; in the context of this royal tableau of corpses, he is king of the dead.

None of these kaleidoscopic "speaking pictures" can be taken as moral or philosophical statements. They are poetic images, open ended, reverberant, ambiguous. The crown is seen to be real, and carries real authority; it may also be utterly without value, or dangerous, blinding, subversive. The very power the crown symbolizes is, in its absoluteness, disastrously linked to infantile fantasy: anyone but a child can see that he is not everything. Yet the crown must be worn.

For discussion, I have isolated the developing images of a symbolic act and of a symbolic thing. In fact, they cannot be separated from each other, as they cannot be separated from the interwoven verbal images. Lear's seeing is one aspect of a total character design that reflects one larger design in the play: the necessity and difficulty of seeing to know. Characters strain to see in the dark, in the storm. Again and again they look off to see what mystery, what danger, approaches. No language is needed to convey to us the persistent alarm as to identity: *What's he? Who's there? What are you there?* One of the oldest techniques of the theatre craftsman, to compel the actors—and hence the audience—to look toward an entrance in anticipation or dread, is repeatedly employed in appearances by Edgar, Goneril, Regan, Mad Tom, Gloster, Gentleman. All actors, like Lear, try to look, see, know. What they see may, in a purely visual stroke, defeat their hopes: most obviously, again, Albany, in a prayerful gesture to the gods, begs Cordelia's safety, Lear enters bearing her corpse. Lear

may die with his eyes open, unseeing, and someone must close them —
a final irony.

Seeing and knowing are never certain in *Lear,* for the play's
dialectic insists on ambiguity. Lear's character design, sustained by
conflicting and even contradictory qualities, emerges in all its
visual manifestations. In a clear light of mime we would see that Lear
sees and does not see. He wishes others banished from his sight, and
he wishes them by him. When sane, he sometimes looks as if mad;
when mad, as if sane. His gestures — as well as his words — would be
qualified by what we see him do: when his refusal to see is frustrated
— as it invariably is — it is associated with another pervasive visual
image: of flight. We saw that men constantly flee pursuit in *Lear,*
but he who flees most is Lear himself, who first ordered Kent to fly.
A mime would stress how much Lear flees, psychically as well as
physically. Lear tries to banish the resistance of others from his
sight, but, failing, he always flees confrontation — until finally
Cordelia has caught him, and they kneel to each other.

Each repetition of a visual image takes on new meaning in a context that becomes more dense and complex as perspectives accumulate. How Lear kneels in serious prayer refracts the implications of
his daughters' initial kneeling to him, of the kneeling of his courtiers,
of his mock kneeling to Regan, of Gloster's blind kneeling to him, of
his kneeling with Cordelia, of his kneeling over her dead body. So
with other symbolic acts, such as putting on or off clothes, weeping,
threatening, playing animal, fleeing pursuit, suffering pain, dying.

These images then, and their associated sounds, support an
organic structure of symbols rich in denotative detail and connota-
tive reverberation and ambiguity, in rhythmic and recurrent patterns and changing perspectives that accumulate and extend the
power of the whole to stimulate feeling, thought, and kinesthetic
response in its audience. They can only be known in performance:
the mind's eye, imagining Lear's physical action, can never recreate
the totality of the visual poetry that the eye's mind, in the theatre,
experiences and organizes.

On the Greatness of *King Lear*

by Stephen Booth

In *King Lear* everything tends toward a conclusion that
does not occur; even personal death, for Lear, is terribly
delayed. Beyond the apparent worst there is a worse suffering, and when the end comes it is not only more appall-
ing than anybody expected, but a mere image of that horror, not the thing itself. The end is now a matter of
immanence; tragedy assumes the figurations of apocalypse,
of death and judgment, heaven and hell; but the world
goes forward in the hands of exhausted survivors. Edgar
haplessly assumes the dignity; only the king's natural body
is at rest. This is the tragedy of sempiternity; apocalypse
is translated out of time into the *aevum*. The world may, as
Gloucester supposes, exhibit all the symptoms of decay and
change, all the terrors of an approaching end, but when
the end comes it is not an end, and both suffering and the
need for patience are perpetual.[1]

The tragedy of Lear, deservedly celebrated among the dramas
of Shakespeare, is commonly regarded as his greatest achievement.
I submit that *King Lear* is so because it is the greatest achievement
of his audience, an audience of theatrically unaccommodated men. . . .

These are the last words of Act IV; the speaker is Kent (all Shakespeare quotations are in the revised Pelican texts, general ed. Alfred
Harbage, Baltimore, 1969): "My point and period will be throughly
wrought,/ Or well or ill, as this day's battle's fought" (IV. vii. 96-97).
This speech, which functions similarly to similar ones in *Julius
Caesar* (V. i. 112-25), *Othello* (V: i. 128-29), and *Macbeth* (V. iv. 16-
21), virtually announces something the play has been telling us for

"On the Greatness of *King Lear*" by Stephen Booth. This selection is composed
of excerpts from work in progress; it is printed for the first time in this volume by
permission of the author.

[1]Frank Kermode, *The Sense of an Ending* (New York: Oxford University Press,
1967) p. 82.

over an hour: as Dover has been the destination of the characters, the inevitable battle there is the destination of the play. At the beginning of V. iii, the last scene, the battle is over, and Lear and Cordelia are led away as captives; they are in urgent danger of death at the hands of Edmund's henchman. When Albany enters with Goneril and Regan, the play is clearly far from over. Although Albany's speech to Edmund ("Sir, you have showed to-day your valiant strain..." V. iii. 40-45), starts out in the standard fashion of victorious generals putting final touches to plays, Albany immediately turns his attention to the object of ours; he demands that Edmund turn Lear and Cordelia over to him. Edmund's smooth answer increases our fears for them; Edmund urged speed on the assassin, and now he says, "they are ready/ To-morrow, or at further space, t'appear/ Where you shall hold your session" (52-54). We fear that Albany may be diverted from his purpose; we have no reason to suspect that we will ourselves forget about the greatest unfinished business of the play. Albany is indeed diverted. He is not taken in by Edmund, but he does forget Cordelia and Lear to challenge Edmund's presumption. Thereupon the play and our attention imperceptibly skew toward the super-imposed love-triangles (Edmund, Goneril, Regan; Edmund, Goneril, Albany):

> *Albany.*   Sir, by your patience,
> I hold you but a subject of this war,
> Not as a brother.
> *Regan.* That's as we list to grace him....
> *Goneril.* Not so hot!...   (59-61, 66)

The focus of our attention now is Edmund, and we are smoothly led into the ceremonial conclusion Edgar has arranged and for which he has carefully prepared us: Edgar's trial-by-combat against Edmund. Edgar's victory, the triumph of virtue, has the feel of dramatic conclusion, and the lines that follow it offer an anthology of familiar signals that a play is ending: Edmund confesses and emphasizes the finality of his situation: "What you have charged me with, that have I done,/ And more, much more. The time will bring it out./ 'Tis past, and so am I" (163-65). Edgar reveals himself and passes a hollow but summary-sounding moral: "The gods are just, and of our pleasant vices/ Make instruments to plague us./ The dark and vicious place where thee he got/ Cost him his eyes" (171-74). The easy readiness of Edmund's agreement ("Th' hast spoken right; 'tis true"-174) combines with the brothers' exchange of charity

(166-67) to give their dialogue a quality comparable to the resolution at the end of a piece of music. Edmund then makes an almost explicit announcement that the dramatic entity is complete: "The wheel is come full circle; I am here" (175). Albany sounds like any one of dozens of rejoicing royal personages tying off the ends of a play by inviting narration of the events leading up to the hero's epiphany (176-83). Edgar's account concludes with information new to us; he tells us once and for all what becomes of Gloucester (194-200).

Edgar's narrative is obviously complete, but five lines later he continues — in a passage whose superfluity the folio text vouches for by omitting it (205-22). He begins on a line that summarizes my point, "This would have seemed a period." This eighteen-line appendix is a chiasmic reprise of Edgar's account of his own activities in disguise (it even echoes the word *burst* and the idea of bursting, which framed the earlier account); here Edgar begins with the events of "some half hour past" and works back to the beginning of Kent's history. This supplementary narrative winds up and ties off Kent's story as the previous one had Gloucester's, and, although Edgar never says that Kent is dead, the parrallelism *does* say so. The Kent story is over. Eight lines later, as the fates of Goneril and Regan are being reported, Edgar says, "Here comes Kent"; Kent enters, and a finished chapter continues.

Kent's first line violently aborts the ceremony of theatrical conclusion that began when Albany called the herald to supervise the formal combat between Edgar and Edmund:

> *Kent.*   I am come
>   To bid my king and master aye good night.
>   Is he not here?
> *Albany.* Great thing of us forgot!...   (235-37)

It seems improbable that the characters could have forgotten about Lear and Cordelia; it seems even less probable that the audience could have done so, but we have. For the audience the smooth ceremony of conclusion collapses only moments before Kent ends it for the characters. As Edgar was putting a precise period to Kent's history, a gentleman entered with a bloody knife:

> *Gentleman.* Help, help! O, help!
> *Edgar.*   What kind of help?
> *Albany.*   Speak, man.

> *Edgar.* What means this bloody knife?
> *Gentleman.*   'Tis hot, it smokes.
>   It came even from the heart of—O, she's dead.   (223-25)

Edgar's questions are our questions and open our minds to a forgotten need for help (note that the gentleman, whose message is
that Goneril and Regan are dead, has no practical use for the help
he asks). The imperfection of the gentleman's response to Edgar's
questioning invites an audience to supply "Cordelia" to complete
the interrupted phrase "from the heart of." When the gentleman
does explain his distress, and when the play ambles on to sum up
the careers of Goneril and Regan, the audience remains upset about
Lear and Cordelia—perhaps not only upset in its concern for two
virtuous characters in danger, but also upset in being the only party
to the play that *is* concerned. Some nebulous uneasiness for the
audience may also result from a sense of having settled itself mentally
in preparation for leaving a theatre where a play has formally concluded while its substance is still in urgent progress.

Even after the characters have remembered that the main business
of the play is unfinished, the audience's travail continues. All the
different plots and subplots have tumbled out on the stage at once,
and the characters leap from focus to focus like the mad Lear of
earlier scenes. The frustration of the audience—which alone can
focus its attention on the one vital action to be taken—is scrupulous-
ly intensified by Shakespeare; his care is epitomized by the paren-
thetic plea for haste with which Edmund delays the syntactic
completion of "quickly send to the castle": "Quickly send—/ Be
brief in it—to th' castle" (V. iii. 245-46).

A moment later: *Enter Lear, with Cordelia in his arms,* and the
most terrifying five minutes in literature have begun for the audience. Throughout his career, Shakespeare risks the mental well-
being of his audiences, exposes his audiences to demands on their
comprehension (ranging in scale from puns and malapropisms to
Shylock and Prospero) by which categories, limits, the very idea of
"kind"—in short the bases of mental well-being—are demonstrated
to be arbitrary, artificial, and frail. At the end of *King Lear* he goes
beyond the mannerist trickery of changing the direction of *Love's
Labor's Lost* in its last moments: Shakespeare has presented an action that is serious, of undoubted magnitude, *and complete;* he now

continues that action beyond the limits of the one category that no audience can expect to see challenged; Shakespeare presents the culminating events of his *story* after his *play* is over.

I submit that audiences are not shocked by the fact of Cordelia's death but by its situation, and that audiences grieve not for Cordelia's physical vulnerability or for the physical vulnerability of human kind, but for their own, our own, mental vulnerability, a vulnerability made absolutely inescapable when the play pushes inexorably beyond its own identity, rolling across and crushing the very framework that enables its audience to endure the otherwise terrifying explosion of all manner of ordinarily indispensable mental contrivances for isolating, limiting, and comprehending.

An audience's experience of the play persistently reflects its characters' experience of the events depicted in it. *King Lear* makes its audience suffer *as* audience; the fact that *King Lear* ends but does not stop is only the biggest of a succession of similar facts about the play. ... Almost from the beginning, both the characters and audience of *King Lear* must cope with the fact that the idea of the ultimate is *only* an idea, a hope, a working convenience. ... To see that the characters constantly and vainly strive to establish the limits of things, we need look at nothing more recondite than Edgar's stoic platitudes in the first lines of IV. i and the revision he offers after the entrance of the newly mutilated Gloucester a moment later (IV. i. 1-9, 25-26). ... Lear's confident reservation of an hundred knights exemplifies a fruitless quest for definition of another sort; his initial scheme and his dream of retirement in a walled prison with Cordelia exemplify yet another; the play is full of them. ...

Not ending is a primary characteristic of *King Lear*. The last sixteen lines of the play provide a brief sample of the varieties of inconclusiveness in *Lear;* an audience's experience of them is emblematic of the experience of the whole. The play began in doubt about who would rule; the three final speeches, a reprise of the division of the kingdom in I. i, leaves us in new doubt about who will rule: Albany? Albany, Kent, and Edgar? Kent and Edgar? Albany and Edgar? Edgar? Other varieties of inconclusiveness are exemplified in Kent's "I have a journey, sir, shortly to go./ My master calls me; I must not say no." It makes literally endless the endless succession of inconclusive journeys in *King Lear;* it echoes Kent's banishment in I. i. and that of Cordelia who said *no*. It also echoes and seems to repeat the substance of the sentence on which

Kent entered this last scene, but where "I am come/ To bid my king and master aye good night" (235-36) said "I come to bid farewell to King Lear, my master, before I die," this speech, where "master" fits both Lear and God, conflates the separated finite world and infinite one referred to in the earlier speech; as a result, the promise of an afterlife acts upon the audience not to put a comfortable footnote to the lives we see ending but to extend our uncertainty into infinity.

These final speeches are also inconclusive theatrically. After the last speech, the folios provide an urgently necessary stage direction: *Exeunt with a dead march.* This is the only one of the tragedies where the last lines do not point to an immediate off-stage destination and invite the remaining characters to repair to it. The last lines of *King Lear* leave the survivors just to walk off the stage.

But my principal reason for focusing on these last sixteen lines is their substance; they dwell on the extreme *length* of Lear's suffering, and, in "shall never see so much," the last sentence comes close to pointing out the audience's parallel ordeal: *King Lear* is too long, almost unendurably so. That sounds like an adverse criticism and ordinarily would be, but it is not so here, where I am arguing that the greatness of *Lear* derives from the confrontation it makes with inconclusiveness. ...

What we ask of art is similar to what Lear asks of life: we ask that art have sure identity, which is to say that it have distinct, self-assertive, limits. ... The last of Lear's statements of despair of Cordelia and hope for her, his death speech, assaults our minds more violently than anything else in the play:

> And my poor fool is hanged: no, no, no life?
> Why should a dog, a horse, a rat, have life,
> And thou no breath at all? Thou'lt come no more,
> Never, never, never, never, never.
> Pray you undo this button. Thank you, sir.
> Do you see this? Look on her! Look her lips,
> Look there, look there—   (306-12)

"And my poor fool is hanged" explodes our confidence that we know what we perceive—just as Lear's death in apparent delusion explodes our hope that his travail will have made him illusion-proof. Lear speaks the line over the body of Cordelia who has been hanged, but "fool" seems a strange choice of words. Although the word "fool" was regularly applied to innocent creatures as a term of pity and/or endearment, although Shakespeare often uses the word to refer to children and to animals ("fool" here is followed immediately by "a dog, a horse, a rat"), and although that information suffices to explain all Renaissance uses of "fool" where the meaning "innocent" is clear from context and a scholarly footnote functions primarily as an historical persuader against student ingenuity, no footnote can dispel the impression that "my poor fool" refers to Lear's Fool. The context that dictates that "fool" refer to Cordelia—Lear's position over her body, the pronoun "thou," her death by hanging, and the echo of two earlier cycles of grief and hope—coexists with the context provided by a play in which one character is a fool, a professional clown, who has vanished noiselessly during Act III, and by a scene punctuated with six reports of off-stage deaths. Moreover, the syntactic habit of the word "and" is to introduce material relatively extraneous to what precedes it; the word appears in a play where such sudden unions of topic are habitual (see I. ii. 23-26, and 111-14, Gloucester's entrance and exit lines in scene two), and is spoken by a character who has been erratically springing from one mental fix to another for five acts. Here again, one sentence, "And my poor fool is hanged," makes two distinct and yet inseparable statements. Our minds are firmly fixed in two places at once. Over and over again in this scene and throughout *King Lear,* an audience thinks multiply —entertains two or more precise understandings at once, understandings that should but do not clash in the mind. Such moments are to the experiences of puns, malapropisms, and our mixed but separable feelings about Hotspur, Prospero, Edmund, or Cordelia as the strength of God is to the strength of Hamlet or Hercules. ...

The strange double reference of "fool" in Lear's last speech is the culmination of a kind of effect that the play achieves in many varieties and from many materials. Each variety and each instance is one in which a mental boundary vanishes, fails, or is destroyed. ... The word "fool" repeatedly fails—is insufficient to define the characters or the kind of behavior to which it pertains, and is inconsistent about the qualities it isolates. ... The Fool himself breaks out of every category in which he might be fixed and out of the play itself. When Kent says "This is not altogether fool" (I. v. 144), we understand that the Fool is no idiot and also that he is no mere joke teller; this is literally an oxymoron—a wise fool, a type beloved in literature, a stock paradox with whom our minds are comfortable. The Fool's first exit speech (I. iv. 306-12) is typical of the traditional character: it is a vatic bon-bon in which the mode is clownish and impertinent and the matter is wise and pertinent to Lear's situation. A real-life professional clown could have been expected to perform a comic routine at his exit; so could a character who is a professional clown. The Fool's double action—as comedian retained by King Lear and comedian performing before a theatre audience—is a single action when the Fool leaves the stage in I. iv. However, where the Fool's first exit from the stage is indistinguishable from his exit from a room in Goneril's house, his next ("She that's a maid" I. v. 51-52) has no audience in the fiction; its substance participates in the thematic undercurrent of sexual wantonness in the play, but it is addressed to and concerns only the playhouse audience. Clowns in plays commonly did and often still do depart from their concerns as characters to fool with the audience. But we have been led to assume that the Fool in *Lear* has abdicated the privilege of ordinary theatrical clowns in order to join the ranks of Tiresias-like fools extraordinary. In the scene concluded by the couplet on maids, the Fool has alternated between showing us sample swatches of the traditional comic material of court jesters and commenting wisely on Lear's folly; he has been consistent to his type, wise fool, a type entirely defined by violations of our expectations about the behavior of fools. When Lear's Fool suddenly talks to the audience like an ordinary fool in an ordinary play, the established paradox of the wise idiot is both capped and deflated in a parallel action whereby the humble seer turns momentarily and unexpectedly into an irresponsible, frivolous clown.

A similar sort of explosion occurs on a larger scale in III. ii, where the Fool's exit lines are to theatrical nature as the storm is to the natural world:

> *Fool* [*sings*]
> > He that has and a little tiny wit,
> > > With, heigh-ho, the wind and the rain,
> > Must make content with his fortunes fit
> > > Though the rain it raineth every day.
> *Lear.* True, boy. Come, bring us to this hovel.
> > > > > *(Exit with Kent.)*
> *Fool.* This is a brave night to cool a courtesan. I'll speak a
> > prophecy ere I go:
> > > When priests are more in word than matter;
> > > When brewers mar their malt with water;
> > > When nobles are their tailor's tutors,
> > > No heretics burned, but wenches' suitors;
> > > When every case in law is right,

No squire in debt nor no poor knight;
When slanders do not live in tongues,
Nor cutpurses come not to throngs;
When usurers tell their gold i' th' field,
And bawds and whores do churches build—
Then shall the realm of Albion
Come to great confusion.
Then comes the time, who lives to see 't,
That going shall be used with feet.
This prophecy Merlin shall make, for I live before his time.

(Exit.)

By delaying the conclusion of the scene, these speeches of the Fool participate in the systematic frustration of our desire to see Lear sheltered, and mirror it by being composed of several superfluous repetitions of a superfluity: the song before Lear's exit fulfills the function of exit routine: "This is a brave night to cool a courtesan" fills it again, and so does the prophecy that follows. These last two also violate the dramatic illusion as the previous exit speech had done, but here the destruction of mental limits and categories extends to time and is more devastating. By definition, a prophecy concerns future time, but in this play all definition is illusory.

Much ingenuity has been expended on the prophecy, but scholarly bridgework is inevitably insignificant and ineffective as compared with the qualities that prompt it—in this case qualities so disturbing that rational men feel called upon to argue the prophecy away or to crush it a little and make it bow to reason. Our immediate response to the first two conditions in the prophecy is that they are not future but present evils: priests who profess more than they perform and brewers who water their beer are chronic. The next two lines are less clear and more disturbing. Just as we recognize the word "bureaucrat" in any modern sentence as a signal that we are expected to feel contempt, a Renaissance audience was conditioned to take *any* mention of dealings between gentlemen and their tailors as an invitation to moral outrage. Moreover, repetition of the *when* construction also suggests that the substance of line three is another current evil similar to those presented by the *when* construction of the first two lines. Line three could be read as a third item in the list of current abuses (nobles know, care, and fuss more about fashion than tailors do) or as a future good (the behavior, values, and opinions of nobles will not be dictated by their tailors), but as the line passes in the theater an audience presumably only feels further disoriented and has no time to speculate on the reason. The fourth line is similar; it is hard to decide—and one has no time to wonder—whether the time when there are "No heretics burned, but wenches' suitors" is present or future, desirable or undesirable. Line four has a cadence-like finality because it breaks from the *when* pattern, but the Fool does not advance to the *then* of his prophecy. The next line makes a fresh start on a fresh *when;* then comes another *no* construction, another *when,* a *nor* construction, a *when ... and,* and, at long last, *then.* Not only does the prophecy duplicate the general pattern of the play by failing to come to a conclusion when it signals one, but our experience with the lines on law, debt, slanders, cutpurses, usurers, and whores are to our experience of the first four lines as our experience of the Fool's suddenly clownish exit speeches are to his apparently fixed character as wise fool. We have just learned that the *whens* of this particular prophecy do not refer to the future but mean "in as much as," "since"; now we get what we are newly weaned from demanding: "When every case in law is right" and five more conditions that are clearly future and apparently desirable. The *then* clause, when it does come, sounds just as prophecy should sound, but *then* has become meaningless. The *then* clause is no more final than anything else in the speech; it is followed by another, in which *then* is also meaningless, although its futurity is underscored, and in which the generic givens of prophecy are obliterated absolutely: we can imagine no time past, present, or future when walking will be done other than with feet.

Now, at last, the prophecy is finished, but the speech is not. We have endured the breaking of the category "fool," the category "wise fool," and the category "prophecy"; now we face the frailty of the category "play." The Fool speaks one more line before he goes, a line of flat prose in which he blows apart the chronological limits of the fiction and, indeed, all divisions between character and actor, character and audience, past and present, past and future, future and present: "This prophecy Merlin shall make, for I live before his time." As the speech went on we tried gamely to get our bearings and hear sense in nonsense, and we are arrived at a conclusion that implies that there are no bearings to get. As an audience of *King Lear* we have cause to cry that we are come to this "stage of fools." We, who are upon the great one, are for the duration of the play at least, aware that any sense we have of our location is false. ...

As the identities of the characters in *King Lear* are both firm and perfectly fluid, so are the bases on which we evaluate them. The play asks us to value faithful service, but we are discomfited when the contemptible Oswald turns out to be as selflessly faithful to Goneril (IV. vi. 250-54) as the Fool and Kent are to Lear, and when the peasant who lunges out of the background to act our will by trying to save Gloucester's eyes prefaces his fatal attack on Cornwall by announcing that he has served Cornwall ever since he was a child (III. vii. 73).

Values that an audience carries with it everywhere but that are not central to *Lear* are also baffled. Stop for a minute and ask yourself in simple-minded terms whether the battle in Act V is won by the good side or the bad side. This is a battle between the French and the English. The French whose "secret feet" have been ominously abroad in the land since III. i lose to "our side," the English. This is a battle between the armies of Goneril and Regan on the one hand and Lear and Cordelia on the other; our side loses. The whole problem is further complicated by Albany—of whom it is said that "what most he should dislike seems pleasant to him;/ What like offensive" (IV. ii. 10-11), and who of all the characters in *Lear* is most like its audience, and who wrestles with and mires himself in the muddle of political and moral values (V. i. 21-27): Albany simultaneously fights against and on behalf of Lear and Cordelia.

In the first few minutes of *King Lear* a Renaissance audience received signals from which it could have identified the kind of play to follow, predicted its course and the value system it would observe (indeed, Edgar and some critics hope that the play that does follow really is of the kind signaled). First, the audience meets a spiritually brutal old man who jokes boastfully about his past whoring. The Gloucester plot is poised to go the exemplary way of its source, Sidney's *Arcadia* (500 pages of lustful strawmen who are crippled by infatuation and brought to grief because they are governed by passion and forget the obligations and aspirations toward which reason beckons them in vain). Any member of a Renaissance audience would have been ready to see Gloucester's subsequent career as a demonstration that "the dark and vicious place" where Gloucester begot his bastard "cost him his eyes," but Shakespeare gave his audience no chance to do so. Our sense of Gloucester's condition changes repeatedly: first we see him as a casually cruel old rake, then in I. ii as a doddering fool, and finally as a pure victim. When Edgar accounts for Gloucester's fate by moralizing the dark and vicious begetting of Edmund, the comment is as insufficient and trivial a summary of what we have seen as it is inappropiate and flat in the dramatic situation in V. iii at the moment Edgar speaks it. Shakespeare so far expands the range in which the characters and their actions ask to be considered that no system for comprehending them can hold them, but he does not let us altogether abandon any of the frames of reference that the play overlays. In Edgar's desperate efforts to classify and file human experiences, Shakespeare tantalizes us with the comfort to be had from ideologically Procrustean beds to which he refuses to tailor his matter.

The strongest signal Shakespeare gave his audience of coming events and the evaluations appropriate to them is Lear's plan to give up rule and divide his kingdom: this play will be another *Gorboduc*. Lear's action will be the clear cause of clear results in which we will recognize another illustrated exposition of the domino theory of Elizabethan politics, the theory now best known from Ulysses' pompous lecture on degree (*Troilus and Cressida*, I. iii. 125-34). ...For an audience brought up to expect reference to chaos when degree is shaked,...Lear's abdication and the partition of his kingdom would have called for commentaries similar to those of *Gorboduc*, but Shakespeare does not provide them—at least he does not provide them in a way calculated to give an audience the comfortable irresponsibility of a secure point of view.

The philosophical platitudes a Renaissance audience learned in school and is ready to apply to *King Lear* are voiced but only as Gloucester's superstitious doddering (I. ii. 101-12). ...Those lines of Gloucester's present all the raw materials of the predictable catalogue of predictable aberrations set off by a violation of the natural hierarchy, but an audience in any period is readier to scorn an old wives' tale of astrological influence than it is to scorn the attribution of a similar chain of aberrations to a precipitating human action with which some of the ensuing events are in a demonstrable cause-and-effect relationship. Gloucester recognizes and articulates the repeating patterns that we ourselves have observed (Lear and his daughters, Gloucester and his sons; Lear and Kent, Lear and Cordelia, Gloucester and Edgar), and will perceive later (the storm will be to the order of physical nature as Lear was when he disarranged the order of society), but Gloucester's organization of our thoughts disorders them, makes us more, rather than less, uneasy mentally, because the kind of comment we expect to hear and the kind of thinking we ourselves are doing are so distorted by the focus and context Gloucester gives them that they function only as evidence of Gloucester's gullibility. Moreover, even that is not quite straightforward because Gloucester joins us in recognizing Lear's blindness about Cordelia but is himself blind to Edmund's wickedness and Edgar's virtue. The only mental satisfaction we have in the scene comes from joining the villainous Edmund in the superiority given him by his perspicuity about the mental weakness of his victim— whose fuddled state and patterns of thought are parodies of our own.

An audience's experience with more purely local ideological stances, stances evoked by the particulars of this particular play, is no easier. For example, through most of scene one we are ready for some summary comment more diagnostically precise than Kent's "Lear is mad." When the observations we have made of the "unruly waywardness that infirm and choleric years bring with them" (I. i. 297-98) are finally given voice, our spokeswomen are the two characters from whom we most wish to be disassociated: Goneril and Regan. 297-98) are finally given voice, our spokeswomen are the two characters from whom we most wish to be disassociated: Goneril and Regan.

Earlier Cordelia has been our agent in labeling the two fairy-tale wicked sisters for what they are. Western culture is genetically incapable of producing an audience not conditioned to identify itself with the youngest of three sisters and to recognize transparent vessels of wickedness in elder sisters pleasing to their parent. In any case, Cordelia's first line, an aside, must inevitably fix her in the bosom of her confidants, the audience: "What shall Cordelia speak? Love, and be silent" (I. i. 62). I am certain that no audience has ever genuinely changed its mind about Cordelia or felt really tempted to do so. That would be considerably simpler than what I believe does happen. When Cordelia's turn comes to bid in Lear's auction, she voices our contempt for the oily speeches of Goneril and Regan and for the premises behind the whole charade. We are relieved to hear the bubbles pricked, but Cordelia's premises do not present a clear antithesis to the faults in Lear's. Her ideas are only a variation on Lear's; she too thinks· of affection as a quantitative, portionable medium of exchange for goods and services (I. i. 95-104). Moreover, she sounds priggish. When she parries Lear's "So young, and so untender?" with "So young, my lord, and true," we share her triumph and her righteousness. We exult with her, but we may well be put off by the cold competence of our Cinderella. We agree with Kent when he says that she justly thinks and has "most rightly said" (I. i. 183), but we are much more comfortable with his passionate speeches on her behalf than we were with her own crisp ones. ...

Even our evaluations of the play are unfixed. Whenever we find
fault with something Shakespeare does in *King Lear*, the alternative
turns out to be in some way less acceptable. The plotting of *King
Lear* invites adverse criticisms, but what Lear says to Kent on the
heath might well be said to anyone who accepts even the more obvious
of the invitations: "Thou'dst shun a bear:/ But if thy flight lay toward the roaring sea,/ Thou'dst meet the bear i' th' mouth" (III. iv.
9-11). Take, for example, the usually disturbing behavior of Edgar,
who seems to be torturing his father by not revealing his identity:
when Edgar at last does reveal his identity, the news kills Gloucester
instantly. The crowning example, of course, is the end of the play—
where we wish events otherwise than they are and where remedy
would give more discomfort than the disease. *King Lear* turns out
to be faithless to the chronicle accounts of Lear, but its perfidy is
sudden; the movement of the plot is toward a happy ending. I expect
that every audience has felt the impulses that drove Nahum Tate to
give *Lear* its promised end and led Dr. Johnson to applaud the deed.
But Tate made wholesale changes; after he had strung and polished
the treasure he had seiz'd, he had a new "heap of Jewels" altogether.
I doubt that many audiences could feel comfortable with a production
that made sensible revision of the ending, but left the play otherwise as Shakespeare wrote it. Rather than fulfill Johnson's prediction
that they would "rise better pleased from the final triumph of per-
secuted virtue," such an audience would probably value finality
above triumph, and echo Kent: "Vex not his ghost. O, let him pass!
He hates him/ That would upon the rack of this tough world/ Stretch
him out longer" (V. iii. 314-16). To allow Lear and Cordelia to re-
tire with victory and felicity would be to allow *more* to occur, would
be to allow the range of our consideration and of our standards of
evaluation to dilate infinitely. It would be a strong man whose natural
ideas of justice and hopes for a happy ending could outweigh his
more basic need—his simple need of an ending—if, instead of Tate,
he had seen Shakespeare.

PART TWO

View Points

Maynard Mack: On Character *

In the light of these backgrounds in romance, Morality play, and possibly archetypal folk motifs, certain identifying features of *King Lear* may, I think, be more clearly apprehended. These features are not peculiar to the play; they are characteristic of Shakespeare's dramaturgy throughout his career; but the lengths to which he here carries them, and their collective effect in combination, do give *Lear* a somewhat special status among the major tragedies, as we may remember Margaret Webster pointing out. One of these features, a clear inheritance from the backgrounds we have been discussing, is the presentation of characters, all of whom have at some time, and some of whom have most of the time, a mode of being determined by what they are and represent in the total scheme of the play rather than by any form of psychic "life" fluctuating among "motives." The life of the Morality character, as Bernard Spivack has ably pointed out, lies in "allegorical" motivation. The character has *esse,* not *Existenz:* "What it does is what it has to do by virtue of what it explicitly and indivisibly is."[1] Morality characters, Spivack notes, continually act out their *esse*, even when it is absurd for them to do so, as when Envy in Medwall's *Nature* puts down his fellow vice Pride with a lying trick for no other reason than that, in his own words, "yt ys my guyse."

The complication in Shakespeare's management of character, whether in *Lear* or elsewhere, is simply that at any given instant characters may shift along a spectrum between compelling realism and an almost pure representativeness that resembles (and evidently derives from) this *esse* of the Morality play, though it is not necessarily allegorical. The growth of Lear's passion in I, iv, culminating in his terrifying curse on Goneril, is conducted with a verisimilitude whose effect in the theatre, it will be remembered, not even Tate could spoil. Edgar stripping down to become Poor Tom, on the other hand, obviously stands very near the pole of representativeness. He acts out for us the forced alienation of the good man (or at least

*From *King Lear in Our Time* by Maynard Mack (Berkeley and Los Angeles: University of California Press, 1965), pp. 66-69. Copyright © 1965 by The Regents of the University of California. Reprinted by permission of the University of California Press.

[1]Bernard Spivack, *Shakespeare and the Allegory of Evil: the History of a Metaphor in Relation to His Villains* (1958), p. 127.

the man more sinned against than sinning) from security and civility in a corrupted world, a theme which is to be repeated almost immediately, in a far more realistic style, in the stocking of Kent, the repudiation of Lear, and the expulsion of Gloucester. Through Edgar we are given the "meaning" before we are given the event. In the successive shifts of Lear's passion during the difficult first scene of the play Shakespeare comes close to balancing the two modes. There are hints of childishness, imperiousness, decaying powers, and incipient fury that the actor may seize on and magnify to give a plausible body to Lear's test of love and consequent folly, but there is also an *esse* in his role which, like that of the Morality hero, *must* present itself surrounded by forces of evil and good to which it is blinded by vanity and passion, *must* make a wrong choice and live to rue it, because that is the lot of man, and man's lot is the ultimate subject of the play.

Shakespearean character often has a corollary peculiarity, which in *King Lear* is allowed a good deal of scope. Its speech, despite the fact that it is often highly individualized, is always yet more fully in the service of the vision of the play as a whole than true to a consistent interior reality. ...

This is precisely the relation that obtains between the character of Lear and his speech to a blind Gloucester in Dover fields about abuses of authority and excesses of sexuality. If we read it back into his *persona*, we wind up in Mr. Empson's position, appalled by an old man's "ridiculous and sordid" obsession.[2] This is particularly true onstage, where if we overstress by gestures and facial movements the psychic "authenticity" of Lear's lament, we lose altogether its emblematic and Morality-based dimension as a meditation or oration in the tradition of *De Contemptu Mundi*, with whose favorite illustration of man's miseries it closes: "We came crying hither. ... When we are born, we cry that we are come To this great stage of fools."

S. L. Goldberg: On Edgar's Character *

Any interpretation of the play necessarily entails an interpretation of the characters, and *vice versa;* the critic can neither dismiss char-

*This selection is composed of excerpts from *An Essay on "King Lear"* by S. L. Goldberg (London and New York: Cambridge University Press, 1974), pp. 41, 115-17, 119-22. Copyright © 1974 by Cambridge University Press. Reprinted by permission of the publisher.

[2]William Empson, *The Structure of Complex Words* (1951), p. 138.

acter as unimportant nor assume that Bradley has dealt with that aspect of the play so thoroughly that he himself can ignore it. On the contrary, he has to ask what the poetry and the total action actually realize *as* character—the precise terms in which it is made real for us and made to matter in the total effect. He requires, that is to say, a conception of character as more than a set of readily nameable moral qualities which motivate an individual's choices and actions in a supposedly pre-existing world. To respond to the poetry fully is to find it expressive of "character" at a far more fundamental level, a level at which we might more accurately speak of "identity" rather than "character" or even "personality." For it consists in a particular, individual way of experiencing, indeed of actually apprehending, reality—or rather, since that may sound too passive, in a particular way of being humanly alive in *and to* the world. In the active manifestation of that life, both the individual's world and his individual self assume a specific reality and a morally significant shape. . . .

Edgar . . . is a true member of the Gloucester family, all of whom in one way or another seem insecure and anxious about themselves, and whose characteristic psychic style is defensive beside the bolder, more challenging, self-confidently active style characteristic of the Lear family. Edgar's decision—it is his first major speech, incidentally, and obviously invites comparison with his brother's first major speech in Act I, scene ii—is quite deliberately taken in order to defend himself (II. iii. 5 ff). . . . All through the play he shows an instinctive skill in the arts of psychic self-preservation, an adeptness not much more engaging when practised on Gloucester's behalf than on his own. But it is important also to notice that self-preservation means more than just saving his life by assuming a disguise. If it were only that, then any effective disguise would do. The curious, striking jump of "and am bethought" might suggest a deeper instinct at work, and it emerges clearly in the second half of the speech. To get to the bottom, where one has absolutely nothing to lose, is to be consciously secure, invulnerable in one's visibly total vulnerability: "The country gives me proof and precedent/ Of Bedlam beggars, who . . . / Enforce their charity." Presented nakedness will "outface" the worst nature can do, partly by challenging its will to "persecute" to complete destruction, and partly by anticipating its will to persecute at all. . . .

. . . Tom's is a world in which ordinary everyday things are not forms of energy as they are for Lear. Although they are simply themselves—material, neutral objects—they can at the same time be "charged," as it were, with a terrifying menace: a menace all the more mysterious and yet all the more real because they are so common-place. ... Human beings are either vessels or victims of "the foul fiend," of a principle of sheer evil so powerful that only one thing is left for men to do: "take heed of the foul fiend," "defy the foul fiend," "prevent the foul fiend," and "bless thee from star-blasting and taking." The world is metaphysically determined; humanity can only suffer its onslaught from without or within. ... The world is essentially unalterable by human action, as though all activity in it were initiated by some evil spirit whose visitations we can in the end only wait to pass by, to be replaced perhaps by a good one. "Pray, innocent, and defy the foul fiend." There is thus the directest line between Tom's wholly negative morality ("obey...keep...swear not...commit not...set not") and Edgar's view that "ripeness is all." Men must endure; even though the foul fiend rages within their hearts, they are essentially acted *upon*. ...

...When it comes to the pinch, he is not so much unable to find anything to say, as unable to restrain the impulse to act. It is already possible to see why Edgar is the most lethal character in the play. Later on, the man who proclaims one moment that he is

> A most poor man, made tame to Fortune's blows;
> Who, by the art of known and feeling sorrows,
> Am pregnant to good pity —   (IV. vi. 222-4)

finds the next moment that (for the best of reasons) he has to kill Oswald. He is the one who (likewise) kills Edmund, and who (like-wise again) kills Gloucester. It is no empty irony that in the storm-scenes he helps to start Lear into madness by suddenly looming in the darkness like an evil spirit. There is a revealing moment in the hovel when Lear asks "this same learned "Theban,"

> What is your study?
> *Edg.* How to prevent the fiend, and to kill vermin.
>
> (III. iv. 161-3)

In Edgar's world as in himself, that disjunction between "prevent" and "kill" is no less clearly marked and (because unacknowledged and unreckoned with) no less devastating than those in Lear's.

Maud Bodkin: On Splitting in Characterization *

In this drama the emotional conflict between the generations is communicated from the standpoint of the old man, the father who encounters in separate embodiment in his natural successors, the extremes of bestial self-seeking, and of filial devotion. Bradley has noted how the play illustrates "the tendency of imagination to analyse and subtract, to decompose human nature into its constituent factors."[1] This mode of thought, he suggests,[2] is responsible for "the incessant references to the lower animals" which occur throughout the play. Thus Goneril is likened to a kite, a serpent, a boar, a dog, a wolf, a tiger. This analysing work of the imagination, separating the bestial and the angelic in human nature and giving them distinct embodiment, in the wicked daughters and Cordelia (and again in Edmund and Edgar, the cruel and the loyal sons of Gloucester), presents another instance of what we have already observed in the "splitting" of the father figure. The splitting in this play is from the point of view of the parent; as, in the Orestes or Hamlet story, it is from the point of view of the child. As, to the feeling of the child, the parent may be both loved protector and unjustly obstructing tyrant, and these two aspects find their emotional symbolism in separate figures in the play; so, to the feeling of the parent, the child may be both loving support of age and ruthless usurper and rival, and these two aspects find expression in separate figures, such as the tender and the wicked daughters of Lear.

C. L. Barber: On Christianity and the Family: Tragedy of the Sacred †

In the first three late romances, Shakespeare turns to dramatizing the fulfillment of the need men have to be validated by feminine presences, now presented as achieved in visionary reunions—reunions

*From *Archetypal Patterns in Poetry* by Maud Bodkin (Oxford: Oxford University Press, 1934), pp. 15-16. Copyright 1934 by Oxford University Press. Reprinted by permission of the publisher.

†This selection is composed of excerpts from work in progress by C. L. Barber; it is printed for the first time in this volume by permission of the author.

[1]*Shakespearian Tragedy*, p. 264.
[2]Ibid., p. 266.

anticipated within tragedy in *Lear* and *Antony and Cleopatra*. In *Lear* the need for a maternal presence is directed onto daughters; Lear's initial abdication amounts, as the Fool says, to his making "thy daughters thy mothers" (I. iv. 175). Regan and Goneril pretend to meet Lear's demand for love in all but incestuous terms (I. i. 74-77). Cordelia defends herself by reference to the norm of human development in the rite of passage of the marriage service:

> Haply, when I shall wed,
> That lord whose hand shall take my plight shall carry
> Half my love with him, half my care and duty.
> Sure I shall never marry like my sisters,
> To love my father all.   (I. i. 101-106)

The relationships towards which the incestuous love tends, to make the daughter a mother, whether by impregnating her, or by depending totally on her, are shown fulfilled in the traditional Christian scenes of the Annunciation and the Madonna with Child — fulfilled in a sacred way that expresses the latent wishes and protects against acting them out, against pursuing in human objects the total fulfillment reserved for divine persons. So a Christian Lear might be provided with the Presence whose lack drives him to madness; his daughters might be spared the demand that they be that presence, that all their tenderness be arrogated to a father who asks them to make him, in effect, their god.

Of course Lear's world is not Christian in this full sense. On the contrary, in the opening acts Shakespeare emphasizes pagan, pre-Christian references. But as we go through Lear's suffering with him, and the sufferings of Gloucester and Edgar, Christian *expectations* come increasingly into play. By the time Cordelia returns, significantly without her husband, we share with part at least of our sensibility the need she comes to meet. As regularly happens in Shakespeare's mature work, religious language comes into play to express the investment in the family bond:

> There she shook
> The holy water from her heavenly eyes,
> And clamor moistened. ...   (IV. iii. 80-82)

What the play presents, however, is not a Christian resolution, but the tragic consequences of this investment.

How fully Shakespeare understood the destructive side of the bonds whose value he so movingly expresses is manifest in his having changed the happy ending of all his sources. The English win, and among the English it is Edmund who has Lear and Cordelia in his power. Lear's great speech in response to that situation (V. iii. 8-21) is often quoted by those who, caught up in the Christian feeling, want to see the play's ending as wholly redemptive, with intimations of a reunion of father and daughter in a hereafter. Lear has undergone a discipline of humility and achieved something like Christian disillusionment with worldly things, together with a sense of the wrong he did Cordelia. He has seen through royal vanity and ceased to care for that part of "everything" he had presumed on ("They told me I was everything; 'tis a lie, I am not ague-proof" IV. vi. 104-105). But he still wants his daughter to love her father all. A chasm of irony opens as we realize that he is leading her off to death. His vision of prison amounts, almost literally, to a conception of heaven on earth—*his* heaven, the "kind nursery" after all.

To talk about what Shakespeare is appealing to, and controlling, in such a moment, one needs to understand the religious traditions or situation he is drawing on, but also the roots of potential religious feeling in the family. For he is presenting the modern situation where religious need, or need cognate to what had been dealt with by worship of the Holy Family, has no resource except the human family— and its extensions in society. ...

Without attempting here to describe the play's extraordinary final effect of affirmation along with tragic loss, the argument I have been indexing needs to be completed by noting that Lear and Cordelia, while they are represented with marvelous understanding as human individuals, also become in effect icons. Lear with Cordelia in his arms is a pietà with the roles reversed, not Holy Mother with her dead Son, but father with the daughter whom he looked to for the divine in the human. In their dramatized lives they are in time, and in the human condition where Lear's demand and Cordelia's sacrifice to it lead to total, tragic loss ("I know when one is dead and when one lives;/ She's dead as earth.") But the realization of them in the theatre takes them out of time, so that there is a kind of epiphany as we finally see them, a showing forth not of the divine but of the human, sublime and terrible as it reaches towards the divine and towards destruction.

Kenneth Muir: On Christian Values *

The play is not, as some of our grandfathers believed, pessimistic and pagan: it is rather an attempt to provide an answer to the undermining of traditional ideas by the new philosophy that called all in doubt. Shakespeare goes back to a pre-Christian world and builds up from the nature of man himself, and not from revealed religion, those same moral and religious ideas that were being undermined. In a world of lust, cruelty and greed, with extremes of wealth and poverty, man reduced to his essentials needs not wealth, nor power, nor even physical freedom, but rather patience, stoical fortitude, and love; needs, perhaps, above all, mutual forgiveness, the exchange of charity, and those sacrifices on which the gods, if there are any gods, throw incense....

Some have thought that Shakespeare, as well as Gloucester, believed that

> As flies to wanton boys, are we to the gods:
> They kill us for their sport.

Others have supposed that he would have subscribed to Kent's exclamation that the stars governed our condition; or, more plausibly, that he would have agreed with Edgar's stern summing-up—

> The gods are just, and of our pleasant vices
> Make instruments to plague us.

But all these, and other, statements about the gods are appropriate to the characters who speak them, and to the immediate situation in which they are spoken. Shakespeare remains in the background; but he shows us his pagan characters groping their way towards a recognition of the values traditional in his society.

Ruth Nevo: On Lear and Job †

The sins of Lear, for which, it is so often held, he is punished, have been indefatigably catalogued. Wicked pride, self-will, self-

*From the Introduction to the Arden Shakespeare edition of *King Lear* by Kenneth Muir (London: Methuen & Co. Ltd., 1952), pp. lv-lvii. Copyright © 1972 by Methuen & Co. Ltd. Reprinted by permission of the publisher and the U.S. distributor, Barnes and Noble, New York.

†From Ruth Nevo, *Tragic Form in Shakespeare* (Princeton, N.J.: Princeton University Press, 1972), pp. 260-61. Copyright © 1972 by Princeton University Press. Reprinted by permission of Princeton University Press. (Footnotes 6, 7, and 8 have been renumbered 1, 2, and 3).

love, vanity, choler, egoism, senile puerility, a crass materialism which views love as a commodity to be bartered and traded, tyranny, sloth, and want of courage, which lays down burdens and offers as rationalization the excuse of old age[1] —all have found their place, severally and together, in the indictment of Lear. And as the indictment grows heavier, the punishment becomes more and more deserved, at the very least justifiable upon Regan's pedagogic grounds:

> O! Sir, to willful men,
> The injuries that they themselves procure
> Must be their schoolmasters.   (II. iv. 304-306)

The play makes Regan the spokesman of this cold self-righteousness, rendering further comment unnecessary. But under any guise, the moral sense which can be stilled by the logic of Job's comforters is probably impervious to tragic experience. Bildadism is so prevalent in the criticism of *King Lear*, I suggest, because the play is a Shakespearean version of the Book of Job, raising the problem of undeserved suffering with a similar insistence, power, and intensity. The Elizabethans saw Job as the pattern of all patience which Lear invokes on the heath; but in the rebellion which is a constitutive part of that ancient contest with God the imagination reared upon the Scriptures could hardly have failed to find the paradigm of what Harbage has so perceptively isolated for comment: "Lear's molten indignation, his huge invective, his capacity for feeling pain."[2]

Like Job, Lear takes his initial prosperity as a sign of heavenly favor; like Job in affliction, he calls the heavens themselves to heavenly account. Like Job, though he die for it, yet will he affirm his own conviction of what injustice is. Like Job, his natural egotism reaches beyond itself to embrace a universe of suffering creatures and returns to the bedrock reality of the suffering creature. Like Job, he refuses to compromise with pain and with evil; refuses to surrender to the plot of optimistic quietism whereby pain and evil are denied, are made into goods, disiplinary or deserved or redemptive; are made nonexistent. Lear, raging in the storm, is no hero of renunciation but of an enormous expostulation; "raging, ravening and uprooting into the desolation of reality."[3] What is dramatized in the action of *Lear*

---

[1]See Lily B. Campbell, *Shakespeare's Tragic Heroes* (Cambridge: Cambridge Univ. Press, 1930), p. 183.

[2]A. Harbage, "King Lear," Introduction, Pelican ed. (1958), p. 27. The Job analogue has also been noticed by J. Holloway, *The Story of the Night* (Lincoln, Nebr.: Univ. of Nebraska Press, 1963), and by John D. Rosenberg, "Lear and His Comforters," *Essays in Criticism* (April 1966).

[3]W. B. Yeats, "Meru."

is the opposite of resignation. It is the way in which an erring man's passionate protest against injustice and humiliation affirms human dignity despite the most relentless pressure of cruelty, cynicism, and degradation that can be brought to bear on it.

L. C. Knights: On the Fool*

The nature of Gloucester's experience is clearly presented, without ambiguity. The Fool, on the other hand, speaks to (and out of) a quite different order of apprehension: his function is to disturb with glimpses of confounding truths that elude rational formulation. At times he seems like something only partly recognized in the depths of Lear's own personality that will not be kept down ("Take heed, sirrah; the whip"), but because he is only licensed, not enfranchised—not, we may say, integrated with the conscious self, which yet has a vein of tenderness towards him—the truth he tells is disguised, paradoxical, sometimes grotesque. He *looks towards* Cordelia, pining when she is banished and slipping out of the play before her reappearance; at the end there is some confusion in Lear's mind between the two (V. iii. 305).[1] Miss Welsford, in the penetrating account she gives of him in her book, *The Fool,* places him firmly in the tradition of "the sage-fool who sees the truth" ("his rôle," she adds, "has even more *intellectual* than emotional significance").[2] The truths he tells are of various kinds. He can formulate the tenets of worldly wisdom with a clarity that worldly wisdom often prefers to blur. He defines the predatory self-seeking of Goneril and Regan, and has a variety of pithy phrases both for the outward form of Lear's mistaken choice and its hidden causes and results. In relation to these last indeed he shows an uncanny insight, pointing directly to Lear's infantile craving "to make his daughters his mothers" (I. iv. 179-81), and hinting at that element of dissociated sexuality that plays into so many human disorders—something that will later rise to the surface of Lear's mind with obsessive force. The world picture

*Reprinted with permission of the publishers from *Some Shakespearean Themes,* by L. C. Knights (Stanford: Stanford University Press; London: Chatto & Windus Ltd., 1959), pp. 108-10, 176. Copyright © 1959 by L. C. Knights.

[1]Professor Kenneth Muir. in a note on this line in the Arden edition, quotes W. Perett—"When Cordelia is away her place as the representative of utter truthfulness is taken by the Fool."

[2]References to Enid Welsford, *The Fool: his Social and Literary History,* are to pp. 253 ff. I am conscious of a very considerable debt to Miss Welsford's promptings.

he creates is of small creatures in a world too big—and, in its human aspects, too bad—to be anything but bewildering. His sharply realistic, commonplace instances—like Tom's mad talk, though with a different tone—insist on the alien aspect of Nature and on all that detracts from man's sense of his own dignity—corns, chilblains, lice, and the mere pricking of sexual desire. The Fool's meaning, however, lies not merely in what he says but in the way he says it—those riddling snatches which partly reflect the moral confusion of the world, but whose main function is to cast doubt on such certainties as the world (including the audience) thinks it possesses. Not only therefore is he an agent of clarification, prompting Lear towards the recognition of bitter truths: it is he, as Miss Welsford insists, who forces the question, What is wisdom? and what is folly? It is through him, therefore, that we come to see more clearly the sharp distinction between those whose wisdom is purely for themselves and those foolish ones—Kent, Gloucester, Cordelia, and the Fool himself—who recklessly take their stand on loyalties and sympathies that are quite outside the scope of any prudential calculus. Like Gloucester, though in a very different way, the Fool is directed towards an affirmation.

Phyllis Rackin: On Edgar: Delusion as Resolution*

Shakespeare seems in *King Lear* to be confronting every possible thesis about the action and its implications with an antithesis, but never allowing a synthesis to emerge. And, as a matter of fact, the very complexity of the issues raised seems almost to preclude their resolution. The attempt to resolve into unity the extremities of hope and despair, virtue and vice depicted in *King Lear* must confront an audience that has seen too much by the end of Shakespeare's play to accept either the easy "poetic" justice of Tate's ending or the perhaps equally easy pessimism that would deny justice entirely. As a result, any attempt at resolution runs a tremendous danger of looking false. Shakespeare avoids this danger, I think, by presenting his resolutions *as* false, at least from certain angles of vision. The results look wonderfully true.

Through Edgar, Shakespeare perpetrates delusions—plays practical jokes—on other characters, and these jokes have the effect of resolving the major issues of the play, even though they never fully

*From "Delusion as Resolution in *King Lear*" by Phyllis Rackin, *Shakespeare Quarterly*, 21 (Winter, 1970), 30-32. Copyright © 1970 by The Folger Shakespeare Library. Reprinted by permission of the publisher.

lose their delusory quality. The first of these delusions, and the most memorable, is the one by which Edgar persuades Gloucester that he has been saved from death by a miracle. Having led the blinded Gloucester to a flat place near Dover, Edgar persuades him that he is at the top of a high cliff. The audience sees that the stage is flat and knows that it represents a flat field. But Edgar persuades his blinded father that it is the high cliff he sought in order to commit suicide. Edgar "trifle[s] thus with his despair...to cure it," for Gloucester's sufferings have made him lose faith in the goodness of the gods and the rationality of the universe: "As flies to wanton boys, are we to th' gods,/ They kill us for their sport." After Gloucester leaps, Edgar, speaking in a changed voice, tells him that he has been miraculously saved from a great fall ("Ten masts at each make not the altitude/ Which thou hast perpendicularly fell./ Thy life's a miracle" and from an evil spirit who led him to the cliff.... What Edgar says, of course, is literally a lie, although symbolically perfectly true. Gloucester has fallen from an enormous height, he has been led by an evil spirit (as he himself later acknowledges: "You ever-gentle gods, take my breath from me;/ Let not my worser spirit tempt me again/ To die before you please!"), and he has been saved by a miracle—the miraculous devotion of the son he repudiated....

Edgar's second trick is played on Oswald. Edgar speaks in a rustic dialect to reinforce Oswald's impression that he is a peasant, and, after killing Oswald, Edgar drops his rustic dialect, opens Oswald's purse, and says,

> Leave, gentle wax; and, manners, blame us not:
> To know our enemies' minds, we rip their hearts;
> Their papers is more lawful.

Oswald's fault throughout has been that he is completely the creature of the social and political hierarchy, unaware of any values beyond worldly status or any code beyond manners. Kent tells Oswald early in the play (II. ii) that a tailor made him, and to emphasize the line, Shakespeare has Kent repeat it for Cornwall [II. ii. 55-62—ed.]. This passage takes its meaning from the symbolic association of "clothes" in *King Lear* with the whole structure of values and practices that govern, protect, and disguise men in society. Oswald is so completely and so merely the creature of the social hierarchy that he serves as a perfect revelation of its limitations. Since he is nothing but clothes, he is inhuman—no less so than the unclothed creature that Lear beholds in the storm. If the poor, bare, forked animal needs clothes to distinguish him from the beasts, the thing made by a tailor lacks even the natural affections that distinguish the beasts from inanimate things. The opportunism that makes Edmund brutal and enables him to betray his own father still lacks, it seems, the sheer deadliness of the pragmatism with which Oswald responds to the sight of the blinded Gloucester [IV. vi. 229-33—ed.]. Oswald sees a human being as a "prize": he is capable of reducing the whole purpose of Gloucester's creation to mechanistic and egotistical terms. Gloucester, to Oswald, is an economic advantage pure and simple.

In view of Oswald's inability to distinguish value from rank, the justice of his death at the hands of a peasant—a person of no rank at all—is very neat. The fact that the peasant is Edgar, dressed in rough clothes and speaking a rustic dialect, complicates the justice and acclimates it to the infinitely complex universe of *King Lear,* makes it, one would like to say, poetic.

The third of these illusions is, in many ways, the antithesis of the second, and in creating it Edgar assumes a shape exactly the opposite of his previous one. He kills Edmund dressed in all the formal splendor that the hierarchy can afford, and again the manner is perfectly appropriate. For if Oswald is too much the creature of society, Edmund is too much its adversary. Edmund's first major speech, a soliloquy, proclaims his defiance of "the curiosity of nations" and "the plague of custom." And it is these things that, in the end, cut him down in the person of his despised, legitimate older brother, dressed in armor and fighting in formal knightly combat. Edmund, like Oswald, is finally destroyed by a representative of all the values he has defied and ignored throughout the play; and in both cases the representation is, at least from one point of view, a delusion.

Nicholas Brooke: On Moral Structure vs. Experience *

The last two Acts of the play, I have suggested, are constructed of a series of advances and repudiations of visions of hope. Each concept is followed by a scene of intense experience to which the idea cannot be applied. Edgar sees his blinded father immediately after

*From *Shakespeare: King Lear* by Nicholas Brooke (London: Edward Arnold Publishers, Ltd., 1963), pp. 58-60. Copyright © 1963 by Nicholas Brooke. Reprinted by permission of the publisher.

claiming that the worst returns to laughter, and learns that "the worst is not So long as we can say 'this is the worst.'" This is a dialectical pattern, of exchange between theory and experience, which is continually repeated. Gloucester's stoic resolution to abjure suicide is followed by sight of Lear too mad for any moral choice. "Ripeness is all" leads to "We two will sing like birds i' th' cage," where no ripeness is possible. The last repetition of this pattern is as simple as the first, when Albany's assertion of poetic justice is met by "And my poor fool is hang'd! No, no, no life!"

One cannot avoid the conclusion that a pattern thus repeated in subtler or cruder forms is essential to the sense of the play. On the larger scale, the reconciliation of Lear and Cordelia that concludes Act IV, and seems finally to endorse the movement towards relief, is met by the whole experience of Act V. It is the unredeemed Lear who boasts of killing Cordelia's executioner; and the excitement of his words must make us pause before wishing that the redemption had been more lasting. It was, in fact, in large part composed of exhaustion; and it ceases to attract, much as "justice" becomes repulsive.

The structural process of Acts IV and V is of course involved in the larger mass of the play. Act I began in the confident richness of the royal pageant; the contrary implications of the solitary Edmund, and the melancholic Fool proceed through the stripping of Act II to Lear's discovery of his own nakedness, "Man's life is cheap as beast's." Act III makes even that seem cheerful; man, exposed like a beast, suffers most i' th' mind. The "clothing" that is removed in the first part of the play is that of traditional assurances of position, home and family; it is replaced in Act IV by a clothing of ideas, of justice and redemption. When that too is stripped in Act V, we are left alone with exhaustion and the relief of death. The concepts fade away, but the naked experience remains. ...

In fact, we may well be moved to feel that the experience is the more vivid because the moral ideas have disappeared. This raises a question about the relation of morality to dramatic experience in the play. I called attention in the prologue to the implausibility of the "plot" abstracted from the play. And in reviewing the structure I often used terms more suggestive of moral allegory than of a compulsive sequence of events. Yet it cannot be doubted that the ultimate quality in the play is the depth of its living experience. It is thus at once the nearest of Shakespeare's plays to allegory, and the furthest from it. Much of the play is very obviously allegorical: Edgar and Gloucester in the last two Acts are the clearest instance. With them, the moral demonstration continually exceeds the dramatic experience, or at least is disproportionately obtrusive. If the whole play were at that level, we might be interested, but we could not be profoundly moved. Yet Lear's scenes are not so widely different: Lear waking in Cordelia's arms, or Cordelia dead in Lear's arms likewise have allegorical significance (I have remarked how often the stage picture is emblematic). The difference between these two is not fortuitous: Edgar's morality play is exposed by Lear's experience; or by contrary, we are assured of the naturalness of Lear's experience partly by feeling its contrast with the demonstrative allegory applied to Gloucester. ...

The final sense is that all moral structures, whether of natural order or Christian redemption, are invalidated by the naked fact of experience. The dramatic force of this rests on the human impulse to discover a pattern, a significance, by investigating nature. But nature itself finally frustrates that impulse; when Lear dies, the moral voices are silenced. We are left with unaccommodated man indeed; naked, unsheltered by any consolation whatsoever. This, one may say, is the function of all tragedy. But it is not a purely aesthetic function; the artistic impulse is to complete a pattern, which is to affirm an aesthetic order, whether its moral equivalent is apparent or not. This, too, *Lear* directly resists: again and again during the last Act we seem to approach the completion of a pattern which might transcend disaster; but each coda is broken off by a renewed sense of its inadequacy, and so again we are left to Lear's deluded death without even the aesthetic consolation of formal patterning.

Chronology of Important Dates

	Shakespeare	The Age
1557		Tottel's *Miscellany* published.
1558		Accession of Queen Elizabeth I.
1561		*Gorbuduc* (first blank-verse tragedy in English) performed.
1564	Birth of Shakespeare at Stratford-upon-Avon (April 23).	
1576		James Burbage builds The Theater, England's first permanent playhouse, in outskirts of London.
1582	Shakespeare marries Anne Hathaway.	
1583	Daughter Susanna born.	
1585	Twins (Hamnet and Judith) born.	
1587		Death of Mary Stuart; *Spanish Tragedy* by Kyd.
1588		Defeat of Spanish Armada.
1590-92	*Henry VI, Parts 1, 2, and 3; Comedy of Errors.* Greene's attack on Shakespeare as "upstart crow" in *Groatsworth of Wit* (first reference to Shakespeare as actor and playwright).	Spenser's *Faerie Queene,* I-III, and Sidney's *Arcadia* published (1590); Marlowe's *Tamburlaine* (1589-90) and *Dr. Faustus* (1592-93).
1593-94	"Venus and Adonis" (1593) and "Rape of Lucrece" (1594) published; *Titus Andronicus, Taming of the Shrew, Richard III, Two Gentlemen of Verona;* Shakespeare joins Lord Chamberlain's Men as actor, playwright and shareholder.	Theaters closed intermittently by outbreak of plague (1592-94).

1595-96	*Midsummer Night's Dream, Richard II, Romeo and Juliet, King John, Merchant of Venice;* death of Hamnet (1596); Shakespeare family granted coat of arms (1596).	Spenser's *Faerie Queene*, IV-VI, published (1596).
1597-98	*Henry IV, Parts 1 and 2;* purchase of New Place (second largest house in Stratford).	Bacon's *Essays* published (1597).
1599-1600	*Much Ado About Nothing, As You Like It, Henry V, Julius Caesar, Twelfth Night.*	Lord Chamberlain's Men construct the Globe Theater from the timbers of The Theater (1599).
1601-02	*Hamlet, Troilus and Cressida, All's Well That Ends Well;* death of Shakespeare's father (1601).	Unsuccessful rebellion by Earl of Essex (1601).
1603-04	*Measure for Measure, Othello.*	Death of Elizabeth and accession of James I (1603); Lord Chamberlain's Men become King's Men.
1605-06	*King Lear, Macbeth.*	
1607-08	*Antony and Cleopatra, Timon of Athens, Coriolanus;* marriage of Susanna (1607); death of Shakespeare's mother (1608).	Midlands riots (1607); King's Men acquire Blackfriar's (private theater with exclusive clientele and evening performances) [1608-1609].
1609-10	*Pericles, Cymbeline; Sonnets* published (1609).	
1611-12	*Winter's Tale, Tempest;* Shakespeare retires to Stratford.	
1613	*Henry VIII.*	Globe Theater burns down during performance of *Henry VIII.*
1616	Death of Shakespeare (April 23).	Jonson arranges for publication of his *Works.*
1623	First Folio edition of plays published; death of Anne Hathaway.	

Notes on the Editor and Contributors

JANET ADELMAN is Associate Professor of English at the University of California, Berkeley. She is the author of *The Common Liar: An Essay on "Antony and Cleopatra."* Her work has appeared in Twentieth Century Interpretations volumes of *Antony and Cleopatra* and "The Pardoner's Tale."

C. L. BARBER is Professor of Literature at the University of California, Santa Cruz. His book on the comedies, *Shakespeare's Festive Comedy,* has been widely influential. He is presently working on a book on the place of the tragedies in Shakespeare's development.

MAUD BODKIN (1875-1967) was a teacher, writer, and lecturer. In her work she attempted to bring together literature, religion, and philosophy through the use of Jungian psychology. Her books include *Archetypal Patterns in Poetry* and *Studies of Type-Images in Poetry, Religion and Philosophy.*

STEPHEN BOOTH is Professor of English at the University of California, Berkeley. His works include *An Essay on Shakespeare's Sonnets* and a forthcoming edition of the sonnets with extensive commentary, as well as essays on individual plays and performances.

A. C. BRADLEY (1851-1935) published his widely influential *Shakespearean Tragedy* in 1904 while he was Professor of Poetry at Oxford University. One of the greatest Shakespeare critics of the twentieth century, he is frequently the point of departure even for those critics who disavow his methods and conclusions.

NICHOLAS BROOKE, Professor of English Literature at the University of East Anglia, is the author of *Shakespeare's Early Tragedies* and the editor of *Bussy D'Ambois,* among other works.

STANLEY CAVELL is Walter M. Cabot Professor of Aesthetics and General Theory of Value at Harvard University. He has written on a wide range of topics of general interest. His works include *Must We Mean What We Say?, The World Viewed: Reflections on the Ontology of Film,* and *The Senses of Walden.*

JOHN F. DANBY (1911-1972) was Professor of English Language and Literature at University College of North Wales at the time of his death. He was the author of studies of Sidney, Beaumont and Fletcher, and Wordsworth, as well as Shakespeare.

S. L. GOLDBERG is Robert Wallace Professor of English at the University of Melbourne. He has written extensively on James Joyce *(The Classical Temper, James Joyce)* as well as on Shakespeare.

G. WILSON KNIGHT, Emeritus Professor of English Literature at Leeds University, has written numerous works on Shakespeare and other authors. His most influential books on Shakespeare are *The Wheel of Fire, The Imperial Theme,* and *The Crown of Life.*

L. C. KNIGHTS, King Edward VII Professor of English Literature at Cambridge University, has written influential essays on character, politics, and other Shakespearean topics. His books include *Drama and Society in the Age of Jonson, Some Shakespearean Themes, An Approach to "Hamlet," Explorations,* and *Further Explorations.*

MAYNARD MACK is Sterling Professor of English at Yale University, Director of the National Humanities Institute, past President of the Modern Language Association and the Shakespeare Association of America, editor of works by Shakespeare, Pope and Milton, and author and editor of many works on Shakespeare and on the eighteenth century.

KENNETH MUIR is King Alfred Professor of English Literature at the University of Liverpool, Chairman of the International Shakespeare Association, editor of the Arden editions of *King Lear* and *Macbeth* and of several critical anthologies, and author of numerous works on Shakespeare, Milton, Wyatt and others.

RUTH NEVO is Professor of English at the Hebrew University of Jerusalem, on the editorial board of *Hebrew University Studies in Literature,* and author of *The Dial of Virtue, Tragic Forms in Shakespeare,* and numerous essays on other subjects.

PHYLLIS RACKIN is Associate Professor of English in the General Honors Program of the University of Pennsylvania. She has written several essays on poetic theory and on Shakespeare, including "Shakespeare's Boy Cleopatra, the Decorum of Nature, and the Golden World of Poetry" *(PMLA,* 1972).

MARVIN ROSENBERG is Professor of Dramatic Art at the University of California, Berkeley. He had written numerous works on Shakespeare in the theater, including *The Masks of Othello* and the forthcoming *The Masks of Macbeth;* he is currently working on a volume on *Hamlet.*

Selected Bibliography

Kenneth Muir's excellent bibliography of *King Lear* in *Shakespeare: Select Bibliographical Guides*, edited by Stanley Wells (London: Oxford University Press, 1973), should be consulted by every serious student of the play. This brief list is merely supplemental to his work. Works discussed in the essays reprinted in this volume are not listed below.

Burckhardt, Sigurd. "The Quality of Nothing." *Shakespearean Meanings,* pp. 237-59. Princeton: Princeton University Press, 1968. A brilliant essay on the mediate vs. the immediate in the characters, experiences, and presentation of Lear and Gloucester.

Chambers, R. W. *King Lear.* Glasgow: Jackson, Son & Company, 1940. A reading of the play stressing the victory of love and refuting more pessimistic critics by pointing out that Shakespeare has mitigated the final horror of the many versions of the *Lear* story in which Cordelia commits suicide.

Clemen, Wolfgang H. *The Development of Shakespeare's Imagery,* pp. 133-53. Cambridge: Harvard University Press, 1951. An examination of the dramatic function of imagery in *Lear,* as well as the implications of particular image patterns.

Colie, Rosalie L. *Paradoxia Epidemica: The Renaissance Tradition of Paradox,* pp. 261-81. Princeton: Princeton University Press, 1966. Emphasizes the fusion and interplay of traditional paradoxes in *Lear,* as well as their nontraditional effect of drawing "the beholder into the experience of contradiction."

Colie, Rosalie L., and F. T. Flahiff, eds. *Some Facets of "King Lear": Essays in Prismatic Criticism.* Toronto: University of Toronto Press, 1974. An excellent collection of essays from diverse points of view.

Coursen, Herbert R., Jr. *Christian Ritual and the World of Shakespeare's Tragedies,* pp. 237-313. Lewisburg: Bucknell University Press, 1976. An extensive discussion of Christian analogues and echoes in *Lear.* Coursen argues that the hints of Christian redemption serve only to underscore the bleakness of the end.

Doran, Madeleine. "Command, Questions, and Assertion in *King Lear.*" In *Shakespeare's Art,* edited by Milton Crane, pp. 53-78. Chicago: University of Chicago Press, 1973. Discusses the significance of these three syntactical forms in creating the world of the play; particularly interesting in noting the relative absence of the conditional except in the speech of the fool, who tries to teach Lear about the world of contingency.

Elton, William R. *King Lear and the Gods.* San Marino: The Huntington Library, 1966. A massive attempt to deny any element of Christian salvation in *Lear* by stressing its pagan elements and the intellectual background that would have made them relevant to Shakespeare's Christian audience.

Empson, William. "Fool in *Lear.*" *The Structure of Complex Words,* pp. 125-57. London: Chatto & Windus, 1951. A quirky and suggestive essay on folly, emphasizing its dark side: Lear as clown and imbecile, and the heavens as fools who make fools of man.

Everett, Barbara. "The New *King Lear.*" *Critical Quarterly,* 2 (1960), 325-39. An analysis of the genesis and consequences of criticism stressing the "reconciliation" at the end of *Lear;* she argues for a view of the play dependent on a tragic valuation of life and its losses.

Frost, William. "Shakespeare's Rituals and the Opening Scene of *King Lear.*" *Hudson Review,* 10 (1957-58), 577-85. An influential discussion of ritualistic elements in I. i and the effect of the breakdown of ritual throughout the play.

Goddard, Harold C. *The Meaning of Shakespeare,* pp. 522-57. Chicago: University of Chicago Press, 1951. An exasperating and interesting essay stressing the primacy of imagination over the senses throughout the play in order to suggest that Cordelia is literally a spirit and that Lear's final vision of her alive is visionary truth.

Goldman, Michael. "The Worst of *King Lear.*" *Shakespeare and the Energies of Drama,* pp. 94-108. Princeton: Princeton University Press, 1972. The book emphasizes the importance of the physical presence of the actors; the *Lear* essay discusses particularly the intensification of pain and the refusal-to-end characteristic of the play.

Granville-Barker, Harley. *Prefaces to Shakespeare,* I, 261-334. Princeton: Princeton University Press, 1946. A thorough refutation of the Lamb-Bradley notion that *Lear* is better suited to the study than the stage; Granville-Barker demonstrates that structure, style, and character work toward specifically dramatic ends.

Heilman, Robert Bechtold. *This Great Stage: Image and Structure in "King Lear."* Seattle: University of Washington Press, 1963. Originally published in 1948, this is the classic study of patterns of image and theme in the play. Heilman traces patterns associated with sight, clothing, nature, justice, values, madness, reason, and the gods. The emphasis is on the redemptive paradoxes of the play.

Holland, Norman N. *Psychoanalysis and Shakespeare.* New York: McGraw-Hill, 1966. A guide to a variety of psychoanalytic interpretations of Shakespeare. Holland's own interpretation of *Lear* emphasizes the importance of masochistic strategies as attempts to buy love by a form of prepayment in suffering.

Kernan, Alvin B. "Formalism and Realism in Elizabethan Drama: the Miracles in *King Lear.*" *Renaissance Drama,* 9 (1966), 59-66. A discussion of Shakespeare's exploitation of the tension between formalism and realism, particularly in Gloucester's mock suicide; Kernan sees this scene as Edgar's morality play in which the "miracles" are partly true but partly undercut by the theatrical absurdity.

Kott, Jan. "King Lear or Endgame." *Shakespeare Our Contemporary,* pp. 87-124. Garden City: Doubleday & Company, Inc., 1964. Despite its exaggerations and omissions, this essay is sometimes suggestive about the affinities of *Lear* with mime and theater of the absurd. It is moreover significant in having helped to shape the conception behind one of the greatest and most controversial stage productions of the twentieth century, the Peter Brook *King Lear.* (For an illuminating discussion of the successes and failures of this production and the interpretation behind it, see V. A. Kolve, "The Modernity of *Lear*," in *Pacific Coast Studies in Shakespeare,* edited by Waldo F. McNeir and Thelma N. Greenfield, pp. 173-89. Eugene: University of Oregon Books, 1966.)

Maxwell, J. C. "The Technique of Invocation in *King Lear.*" *Modern Language Review,* 45 (1950), 142-47. One of the earliest essays to trace the ways in which each character's "religion" reflects his own nature, as well as the progress of Lear and Gloucester toward Christian attitudes.

Stockholder, Katherine. "The Multiple Genres of *King Lear:* Breaking the Archetypes." *Bucknell Review,* 16 (1968), 40-63. A study of the tensions produced by the elements of fairy tale, farce, and satiric comedy that combine with tragedy in *Lear.*